EVERYDAY CALMING
RITUALS

TRIGGER™

The mental health & wellbeing publisher

ABOUT THE AUTHOR

Tania Ahsan is a former journalist, who has previously edited *Kindred Spirit* magazine. She is the author of *The Brilliant Book of Calm* and *Declutter Your Life: From Chaos to Calm*. She practises daily rituals and meditation in order to increase her own sense of calm, and teaches these methods to companies and organisations in the UK and Ireland. She is considered a Mind, Body, Spirit expert and continues to write and publish extensively in this area. She lives in south London with her serene husband Gary and lots of grumpy, high-maintenance plants.

BY THE SAME AUTHOR

The Brilliant Book of Calm (Infinite Ideas, 2008)
Declutter Your Life: From Chaos to Calm (Infinite Ideas, 2012)

EVERYDAY CALMING RITUALS

SIMPLE DAILY PRACTICES TO REDUCE STRESS

TRIGGER™
The mental health & wellbeing publisher

First published in 2020
This edition in 2023 by Trigger Publishing
An imprint of Shaw Callaghan Ltd

UK Office
The Stanley Building
7 Pancras Square
Kings Cross
London N1C 4AG

US Office
On Point Executive Center, Inc
3030 N Rocky Point Drive W
Suite 150
Tampa, FL 33607
www.triggerhub.org

A CIP catalogue record for this book is available upon request from the British Library
ISBN: 978-1-83796-342-3
Ebook ISBN: 978-1-83796-343-0

Cover design by Bookollective
Typeset by Lapiz Digital Services

Trigger Publishing encourages diversity and different viewpoints. However, all views, thoughts and opinions expressed in this book are the author's own and are not necessarily representative of us as an organization.

All material in this book is set out in good faith for general guidance and no liability can be accepted for loss or expense incurred in following the information given. In particular this book is not intended to replace expert medical or psychiatric advice. It is intended for informational purposes only and for your own personal use and guidance. It is not intended to act as a substitute for professional medical advice. The author is not a medical practitioner nor a counsellor, and professional advice should be sought if desired before embarking on any health-related programme.

DEDICATION

For my mother, Farah, with love and gratitude always.

CONTENTS

INTRODUCTION

*"... I do believe that if your culture or tradition
doesn't have the specific ritual you are craving,
then you are absolutely permitted to make up a
ceremony of your own devising ..."*
Elizabeth Gilbert, *Eat, Pray, Love*

Do you perform rituals? You may categorically answer 'no', but what about blowing out the candles on your birthday cake once a year or catching the bouquet at your friend's wedding, or the solemnity with which you sat through your grandfather's funeral service? Rituals are actions that you do in order to intentionally honour your connection to someone or something. This might be your family, your friends, your community, your religion, your nation or any group you choose. In this book, I'm sharing a different kind of ritual with you – those that honour your connection to *yourself*.

WHAT IS A RITUAL?

In recent years, glossy magazines have started referring to beauty treatments as "rituals" and this ties in to the notion that you are pausing and intentionally honouring yourself rather than just trying to look good. You are consciously nurturing yourself with that hair oil treatment or that pedicure, not just trying to make yourself Instagrammable.

We understand a ritual to be something that elevates an everyday action beyond the mundane to a sacred space. If you light a candle because of a power failure, it feels very different to lighting one to sit in front of in meditation. It is our intention that gives our actions meaning, so the definition of ritual that I am using in this book is any act that is done with the purpose of making the everyday into the special. It is the intention you set, the space and time you put aside to perform the act, and the way it makes you feel afterwards. I believe anything can become a ritual if it is done with intention, awareness, and mindful respect. For example, when you take the dog for a walk, it is elevated to the state of a ritual if you use the opportunity to connect not just with your furry pal but also with your own role as a care-giver to your dog. If, instead of rushing out to the nearest bit of green and scrolling through your phone waiting for him to do his business, you really engage with him and maybe throw a stick and take some time to play and connect, this becomes a ritual. You can even elevate the picking up of dog poo to a higher level by remembering that by doing this you are looking after your pet *and* looking after your neighbourhood.

Now I'm not suggesting that every little thing you do becomes ritual; that would be odd and, in the case of Obsessive Compulsive Disorder (OCD) sufferers such as myself, it could become unhelpful. Instead, I'm suggesting that you introduce rituals into your life that you can then call on when you're in the midst of panic, stress, and anxiety. Rituals that can really help in calming your nerves, bringing you back to your breath, and reminding you that it will all be okay.

I discovered the benefits of rituals when I was a magazine editor for one of the world's largest media corporations. I was doing 15-hour days, taking work home, working at weekends, and feeling utterly miserable. What was worse was that, paradoxically, I was editing a magazine – not *Kindred Spirit*, I hasten to add, which was always lovely to do! – that regularly covered mindfulness and spiritual connection. Mindfulness is the practice of becoming aware of yourself, your thoughts, and the world around you without judgement and with acceptance. It has been found to be profoundly calming when it is done right, as you will see in this book. I, regrettably, was not doing it right.

One night – still in the office at 9 pm – and in the midst of editing a feature on finding joy in everyday things, I had a panic attack. I could feel my chest tightening and I was convinced I was having a heart attack. However, somehow in the back of my mind I knew that this wasn't a cardiac issue, it was a stress response. I had edited enough articles on the subject to know what I was doing wrong. Instinctively, I put my head on my desk and breathed in deeply. I could smell the paper that was beside my head. I could feel the cool of the laminate of the desktop against my cheek. My eyes, blurry with tears, could nevertheless see the different coloured papers in that stack on my desk – the layers of magazines, printouts, invoices, and budget sheets. I could hear – or perhaps feel – the whir of my computer working on the desk. In breathing in and out gently, I began to feel my chest loosening and, as I raised my head from the desk, my tears fell down to my mouth where I could taste the salty reminder that something had to change. It was the taste of being bullied in the school playground and I was being taken back there.

After that, I began to watch myself more closely for clues as to what could help me and I started doing the head-on-desk ritual more often both in the evenings and during the day – although unfortunately a daytime "head on desk" looked to everyone else as if I were having a nervous breakdown (which wasn't that far from the truth).

I began using my senses as a bit of an emotional first-aid kit to bring me back to my body, stop my mind racing with untrue and distressing thoughts, and to remind me that there was a greater world than that within the office. A pal at my last workplace would pick up a pretty leaf on her way into work and keep it on her desk all day long: she said it was to remind her that in the midst of a stressful

"I began using my senses as a bit of an emotional first-aid kit to bring me back to my body, stop my mind racing with untrue and distressing thoughts ..."

work day, the world continued outside with all its beauty and serenity untouched by the small dramas of our lives.

THE POWER OF THE SENSES

In calming myself down, I was focusing on something that we all have – our senses. Even if you're without one or two of your senses, odds are you will have the others.

Elementary school children are taught about five senses, but, in fact, scientific studies now believe we have anywhere between fourteen and twenty-one. This might seem strange to you, but there are a whole host of senses involved in letting you know where one part you ends and where other parts of you begin, as well as directional senses that enable you to know when you are walking forwards as opposed to walking backwards. Then there is your sense of balance and hunger and thirst, all receptors that give messages to your brain and are considered to be senses.

The senses we will concern ourselves with in this book are the five that Aristotle outlined in *De Anima* (*On the Soul*) – sight, sound, smell, taste, and touch. Rituals grounded in your five senses are easy to perform because you are concentrating on a power you use every day and are familiar with. It may be that over the years you have stopped honouring a particular sense because you have felt as though it wasn't as necessary to your life as another one; this book will help to bring you back into balance. For example, has it been years since you've really smelt something that made you feel overwhelmed with desire or happiness? Have you been too busy using your sense of sight at work and your hearing on the commute to and from work? Perhaps it is that very commute that has led you to try to dampen your sense of smell so that it isn't too unpleasant?

On the other hand, have you ever gone into a massage therapist's room feeling tightness in your muscles and with a racing mind, and then emerged an hour later so relaxed you're almost asleep? The best massage therapists aim to stimulate the five main senses in order to create a healing experience; they elevate ordinary acts into the extraordinary through the use of ritual. They may put a flower floating in water under the face hole of the treatment table so that if your eyes are open, you can see something beautiful. The cloth on the table might be a beautiful batik in calming colours. There is usually the smell of essential oils and in an aromatherapy massage you will be asked to select the scent that appeals most to you. You can hear soothing music or sounds, such as ocean waves or birdsong. Long strokes of the therapist's hands, wrists, and elbows across your bare back ease out all the aches and tensions. At the end of the session you are often given herbal tea to drink to further the effects of the experience.

What is happening there? All your senses are being appealed to in order to remind you that you are in a healing space and can leave your worries and concerns at the door. Your brain reacts to all this input and complies with the instruction to relax. You do not have to spend a fortune on massages to gain this experience in everyday life and to train your brain to know when to calm down. The rituals in this book will enable you to take yourself

"The rituals in this book will enable you to take yourself into that healing space. They will provide a counterbalance to our busy, hectic lives by giving us a reason to pause, slow down, and focus on self-care with intention."

into that healing space. They will provide a counterbalance to our busy, hectic lives by giving us a reason to pause, slow down, and focus on self-care with intention. They will keep you calm and centred so that you are not buffeted by emotions day to day.

HOW TO USE THIS BOOK

You can either dip in and try the rituals that most appeal to you or work your way through the book chronologically. I would recommend choosing at least one ritual from each chapter so that you can honour each of

BRAINWAVES

Everything you do, think, and feel affects your brainwaves – the electrical pulses from neurons communicating with each other. Brainwaves change in frequency from slow to fast. When you are in a state of anxiety, you are likely to be experiencing beta waves (12 to 38 Hz) – the brainwaves of everyday consciousness. It is not to say that this is a bad state for your brain to be in, as we need to be alert enough to get things done and function. However, through ritual, we attempt to move the brain into alpha (8 to 12 Hz) and even theta waves (3 to 8 Hz). These deeper meditative states fall on a spectrum from a quiet awareness of being "in flow" to deep meditation, where everyday concerns fall away and you turn inwards to view your own thoughts like clouds passing across a sky.

your senses. If for any reason you don't have a particular sense, you will still find plenty in the chapters on the senses you do have.

The most important part of any ritual is setting an intention – explicitly stating what you want to achieve by doing the ritual. I have suggested an intention for each ritual, but really make the process personal to you by devising your own. Make sure your intention is present and positive so, for example, it would be: 'I create a scene that relaxes me and makes me happy' rather than 'I will not be stressed when I look at this scene'. Do you see the difference? 'I will be' is in the future rather than in the present and 'not be stressed' is not the same as 'relaxes me and makes me happy'. Always aim to be present and positive.

PREPARING FOR RITUAL

There are preparation notes for each ritual, including a list of items you'll need. Also bear in mind these general points:

- Make sure you are physically well. If you are ill, rest, remember to drink your daily intake of water, and return to your rituals when you are back in good health.
- Wear loose or comfortable clothes that don't restrict your breathing or ability to move.
- Have a light snack and a drink before you start so that you are not hungry or thirsty, but don't eat a heavy meal as that will leave you feeling sleepy and lethargic.
- Turn off or silence any gadgets (unless one of the rituals uses them).
- Ask your family to give you the time you need to do the ritual and not to disturb you if at all possible.

THREE BREATHS

Every ritual in this book begins with three cleansing breaths. This is to remind you that you are about to enter into a sacred space and so that you can begin to train yourself to feel immediately calmer. In time, when you are out and about during your day and begin to feel stressed, you will be able to use this three breaths technique to calm yourself down – even if it is not followed by a full ritual. The breathing with intention itself becomes a mini-ritual.

Breathe in and out through your nose as this slows down your exhale and draws more oxygen into your body. Nasal breathing has been shown to be more efficient at promoting blood flow and fighting infections. It helps maintain body temperature and improves some brain function and has been shown time and time again to be great at putting the brakes on stress.

When taking the three breaths, don't rush. Just gently breathe in through your nose, feeling your chest expand, and out through your nose, feeling your chest compress. Place your hand on your belly and try to feel your breath affecting it rather than just stopping in your chest. You may find that you do more than three breaths, once you begin. This is not in any way "wrong" or problematic. Learn to connect with your body so that you know what is right for you. Just be sure to go nice and slow as fast, shallow breathing can lead to hyperventilation (overbreathing).

YOUR RITUALS JOURNAL

If you're anything like me, you'll have a whole shelf of blank notebooks that you've been gifted or that you've squirrelled away after raids to stationery shops. If not, you will have the pleasure of buying one. Find a notebook that most appeals to you: it doesn't have to be expensive, but do pick one that feels right to you. Ensure it is large enough for extended writing and the occasional doodle if you are a more visual person. As you go through the rituals in this book, you will find journal prompts to help you get the most out of what that ritual meant for you. It is a really handy record to look over when you are further along in your journey. It will also give you a better understanding of yourself and your needs.

After using rituals for a while, and becoming more self-aware through journalling, I did, eventually, literally "come to my senses" and quit my stressful job. I remained in the field of editing Mind, Body, Spirit magazines and books, but this time I was actually listening properly to the authors and writers I commissioned and interviewed.

RITUALISE IT

At the end of each ritual, there is a suggestion for how often you should do the ritual to gain maximum benefit. Again, this is just a suggestion so don't beat yourself up about not doing a particular ritual regularly. The last section is on daily, weekly, monthly, and seasonal rituals that show you how to move into a space of calm when dealing with the stresses of obligations that we all have. This should inspire you to create your own rituals based around the occasions that you need them most. In working with your senses, any time you start to feel stressed and anxious with everyday life, you can step outside that feeling by regularly turning to the ritual or rituals that most resonate with you. You will find that your capacity to make that step increases the more you practise.

1

SIGHT

"The only thing worse than being blind is having sight but no vision."
Helen Keller, author and political activist

It is the miracle of sight that enables us to feel calmed by looking at a beautiful azure sea, experience the wonder of brilliant virgin-white snow, and judge when fruit is ripe simply by looking at it. These feats of sight are only accomplished because our brains fill in the gaps and interpret what we are seeing, which enables us to recognise an object from its surroundings, understand distance and depth perception (only made possible because we have two eyes rather than one). An article in the science magazine *Discover* stated that seeing "is a form of sensory reasoning ... Everyday vision encompasses an extraordinary range of abilities ... We see colour, detect motion, identify shapes, gauge distance and speed, and judge the size of faraway objects. We see in three dimensions even though images fall on the retina in two. We fill in blind spots, automatically correct distorted information, and erase extraneous images that cloud our view (our noses, the eyes' blood vessels)."

SUPER-SENSE

Around 80% of our sensory impressions come to us through our sight, which is the most powerful and complex of all our senses. In millionths of a second, light enters the lens of the eye, hits the retina, and is interpreted by the brain. We are born with full-size eyes, which begin to develop from just two weeks after conception. Using the simple palette of three colours – red, blue, and yellow – our eyes create millions of colour combinations and enable us to see a whole spectrum of light.

> "Our ability to conjure up images in our 'mind's eye' is just one part of the tremendous toolkit we have at our disposal to see our way into a better experience of life."

The magic described here is something that we all take for granted on a daily basis. We can, however, re-enchant ourselves and start to love the beauty of the world around us by using sight in the rituals of daily life. Our ability to conjure up images in our "mind's eye" is just one part of the tremendous toolkit we have at our disposal to see our way into a better experience of life.

"WATCHING" TV

When I was a child, growing up in Pakistan, we had one TV – a black-and-white set – that had one channel and only showed programmes in the evenings. There was one children's programme on once a week. As such, to watch TV was a real pleasure, a weekly ritual of joy more akin to going to the cinema than flipping a switch unthinkingly, and the TV was never on as background noise. The family would all gather around to watch a programme and, for the majority of time that it was off, the TV had its own delicate lacy cover, which meant it never got dusty. When someone died, even if it was a neighbour, the TV would remain off for 40 days to show respect to the mourning family members. It remained turned off, no matter how much I pleaded with my grandfather to let me watch my weekly TV programme with the volume turned down low. The TV was a source of intense pleasure, a licentious saucepot that could only be allowed to provide entertainment if all the family were present and no one had died in the locality.

This will seem very archaic to some readers, especially when you consider how we treat our TVs now. One of the first things many of us do when we get home is switch the TV on. Rather than being a mere object, the TV becomes company, even part of the family, especially for those who live alone. The old rituals that focused on gathering around a screen are no longer followed. With streaming now prevalent, families rarely gather together to watch a TV programme, unless it is a special occasion such as the Super Bowl in the US or "The Queen's Speech" on Christmas Day in the UK. There are often multiple TVs in a home and the family might watch different programmes in different rooms; some household members might watch on their tablets or phones. Even if we do sit with our family in front of the TV, doubtless several of us will be on our phones scrolling through social media or on our laptops catching up on work.

How do we regain that feeling of TV-watching as a special privilege, a treat for the senses rather than a numbing constant presence?

It may sound counterintuitive, but try going a month without watching any TV. I know this is tantamount to heresy for some, but it really works.

"Everyday calming rituals are not about a monastic turning away from all technology and the things you enjoy. In fact, they are about enjoying them even more, just consciously and with all your senses engaged."

A friend of mine broke her TV when she was moving house and since she wasn't insured, she couldn't buy a new one until her next payday. She told me that watching that first TV programme when she got her new set was something special. She made some snacks and settled down on the sofa to catch up on a boxset she loved and had missed. She was entirely present and enjoyed every minute. This is a good example of the sort of thing I would like you to pay attention to – everyday calming rituals are not about a monastic turning away from all technology and the things you enjoy. In fact, they are about enjoying them even more, just consciously and with all your senses engaged.

THE BENEFITS OF SIGHT RITUALS

Our eyesight provides so much of the information that we get about the world around us. Rituals involving this sense can help us to appreciate the beauty and wonder that surrounds us and come alive to the possibility of new vistas opening up, literally and metaphorically, in our lives. Apart from trying the specific rituals given in this chapter, pay close attention to what your eyes are telling you about your life and how you are experiencing it.

SIGHT TIPS

- Do you take care of your eyes? Ensure you have regular check-ups and, if you do a lot of screen work, keep moisturising eyedrops handy.
- Make a note in your rituals journal (see page 10) of the best sights you have ever seen. This might be the first moment you saw your newborn baby or the incredible sights from the top of a mountain you climbed.

Note how that sight made you feel and also note down any other senses that came into play such as smell or sound.

- Make a conscious effort each day to look for three things that you see that fill you up with a sense of joy and wonder. It may be the intricacies of a fallen leaf or an impressive church or temple, or perhaps noticing the beautiful eyelashes of a loved one asleep and peaceful. Make a note of them in your journal.

Visualisation

"You can't depend on your eyes when your imagination is out of focus."
Mark Twain, author

Visualisation works. How do we know? Several studies have found that professional athletes activate the same brain patterns when they are imagining doing their sport as when they are actually doing it. So it seems that a key part of preparation for professional sports is visualising ever-greater success.

A vision board is a great tool for visualising what you want to manifest. Some people use one to manifest material things, such as greater abundance, or personal goals, such as a loving relationship, but it can also be used to create an instant reminder of what it feels like to be calm and in control. Then, when difficult feelings of panic and overwhelm arrive, you can remind yourself of what it feels like to be relaxed and serene.

A vision board gives you an instant way to focus on positive images. Think about why so many people watch dramas set in beautiful locations, such as the Caribbean or the Scottish Highlands. The scenery takes us out of our everyday lives and allows us to be "transported" to that place. Tourism often increases in a beautiful location when it has been featured on TV. We are often shown places in their best light, with great weather and quaint architecture, when the truth might be that it usually pelts down with rain and there are concrete shopping malls. It is not the reality that appeals to us, it is the fantasy. For the same reason, I love watching schmaltzy US teen dramas about mermaids. The colours the film-makers use are hyper-real – bright, with shimmers and sparkles that you only get to see in magical TV productions and rarely in nature.

RITUAL

Making a vision board

Vision boards capture the fantasy for us to look at whenever we need a boost. The ritual of making a vision board ensures that the feeling it gives us will always be real, even if the place we've created on the board isn't. This ritual enables you to identify the images you want to see to achieve peace, calm, and positivity. You can create a scene to turn to when you're feeling stressed or negative and unmotivated. As you get more proficient, you can create ever-more specific vision boards to manifest those scenes into your life.

PREPARATION

The absolute key to this ritual is to do it when you have enough time, so don't attempt it in the half hour before the school run or squeeze it into an evening when you're feeling tired. Ensure that you have scheduled a good hour to yourself. This should be an enjoyable exercise rather than a chore, and you should take some time to set the mood properly. Ensure you have a tidy work surface and that your sightline isn't filled with things that will distract you from the task at hand (move that pile of ironing or that tray of bills waiting to be paid). If you can do this ritual in a private room, all the better. If not, ask your family to give you a bit of space and time and to not interrupt you. Try to switch off the TV so there are no visual distractions. Put some gentle music on if you feel uncomfortable with complete silence.

You will need:
Candle
Pen
A3 card
Old magazines or images printed from the internet
Paper glue

INTENTION

I create a scene that relaxes me and makes me feel happy.

RITUAL STEPS

1   Light a candle and allow your eyes to enjoy the sight of the flickering flame. Try to relax your eyes so that your vision goes a little blurry.

2 Sit on a straight-backed chair at a table or desk and keep your feet flat on the ground.

3 Take a deep breath in through your nose, hold for a couple of seconds, and then exhale through the nose, gently but with control.

4 Take two more breaths like this and, each time, relax your body a little more.

5 Open your eyes fully and settle yourself down to begin making your vision board. You may want to say your intention out loud at this stage, if it helps you to focus. Use the example above or write your own.

6 Write a word in the middle of the A3 card. The word should represent what you most want to feel when you look at your vision board later. Examples might be "calm" or "happy" or "inspired". If you prefer to just have images and no words on your board, that's also fine. This is *your* ritual so make your own rules around it.

7 Look through the old magazines or printed internet images and find those that particularly appeal to you and relax you. It could be images of beautiful beaches or a stunning sunset or a wooded glen. Free holiday brochures are a great source for this.

8 Cut out the images you like best and glue them around the central word on the card. Get creative and add as much as you fancy to it. You can buttress an English wood against a Caribbean beach if this combination would be your absolute fantasy perfect place to feel relaxed in.

JOURNAL REFLECTIONS

Use your journal to reflect on how you felt during the ritual. Which of the images you have selected really make you feel relaxed when you look at them? Is it the sight of clear blue water? Or a shiny sink empty of dishes? Perhaps a hill of untouched, pristine white snow? Why does a particular image appeal to you? Does it remind you of a time that you felt particularly calm? A holiday perhaps or a time when you felt in control? Make as detailed notes as possible – who were you with at the time? What were you doing? How were you living? What has changed to draw you away from that scene now? Perhaps you've never experienced it in real life and it is a fantasy image for you. How would it feel to see this sight every day? Remember, this is personal to you so perhaps those things that most people find relaxing such as images of a Buddha or the sea do not evoke that for you due to your own personal experiences (for example, someone who was in Bali during the 2004 tsunami might not find those images relaxing any longer). Perhaps you prefer the image of a cave or a hobbit house where you would feel protected and secure? Make a note of the sights that most say "peaceful", "relaxed", and "happy" to you.

RITUALISE IT

Make a note in your diary to make a vision board every three months. When I began doing this ritual, I was shocked at how often the images I had used had mysteriously manifested for me in the months that followed. As you start to review your vision boards over time, reflect on how things have changed and how you might focus with more intention on what you would specifically like to manifest. You could create a mini-vision board that you can take out and about with you, and you can definitely create more than one, but do the full ritual for making the board each time and don't make them on the same day. This isn't a speedy activity on your crowded to-do list, so it is something to schedule once a quarter – much more pleasant than doing quarterly accounts! You should do this with intention so that you can really feel the sense of calm you are trying to invoke when you look at it in future.

DAILY BENEFIT

Having created this board with intention, put it somewhere you will see it every day. I keep mine taped inside my wardrobe door so I can see it first thing in the morning and last thing at night. Whenever you need to – daily, if necessary – you can turn to it for a feeling of calmness.

VISUALISATION MEDITATION

If you're not in a position to make a vision board, you can gain some of the same benefits by doing a regular visualisation meditation. You can either buy a pre-recorded guided meditation or you can do your own. Simply close your eyes, take three deep breaths in and out through the nose. Let your mind wander to a scene that you find relaxing and stay there a while. Visit your "happy" place as often as you can and fill in details. For example, if you're walking down a stretch of beach you love, imagine what your feet look like scrunching sand between your toes. Hear the seagulls. Smell the brine in the air. Pick up a seashell and notice its pretty patterns and the way the sun bounces off it. When you are ready to come back, rub your palms together briskly before opening your eyes and returning to the room.

Art

"In other words, the unique value of the 'authentic' work of art has its basis in ritual, the location of its original use value. This ritualistic basis, however remote, is still recognizable as secularized ritual even in the most profane forms of the cult of beauty."
Walter Benjamin, cultural critic and essayist

Walter Benjamin believed that an original work of art has what he termed "authenticity" – it is anchored in the time and space of when and where it was created as well as in the place it ends up, be that a gallery or a collector's home. A reproduction poster of an artwork, no matter how lovely, lacks the authenticity of its original, which is why we value original works of art so much more than even very exact replicas. It is also for this reason that this particular ritual requires you to leave the comfort and safety of your home (unless you are fortunate to have an original artwork at home) and get out to view some art.

Find the original if it is in your city – or other works by the same artist if that particular piece is abroad and currently out of reach. The artist Georgia O'Keeffe made people see the extraordinary in the ordinary with her intense magnified paintings of flowers. Her decision to look very carefully and infinitesimally at something so everyday changed the way we look for those viewing her art. "If I could paint the flower exactly as I see it no one would see what I see because I would paint it small like the flower is small. So I said to myself — I'll paint what I see — what the flower is to me but I'll paint it big and they will be surprised into taking time to look at it — I will make even busy

New-Yorkers take time to see what I see of flowers." This element of surprise you get by playing with the size of things is something you can incorporate into your life by looking closely at things and then imagining what they might be like at a far larger size.

Alexandra Horowitz in her book *On Looking* attempted, through eleven walks taken with others (including her dog, her toddler, and a variety of experts such as an artist, a naturalist, and a geologist), to look at her daily walk in her local neighbourhood anew. She wrote of the experience: "I would find myself at once alarmed, delighted, and humbled at the limitations of my ordinary looking. My consolation is that this deficiency of mine is quite human. We see, but we do not see: we use our eyes, but our gaze is glancing, frivolously considering its object."

When taking a walk with artist Maira Kalman, Horowitz muses on the similarities between the way a child looks at the world and the way an artist does – how both look without immediately categorising what they see: "The artist seems to retain something of the child's visual strategy: how to look at the world before knowing (or without thinking about) the name or function of everything that catches the eye. An infant treats objects with an unprejudiced equivalence: the plastic truck is of no more intrinsic worth to the child than an empty box is, until the former is called a toy and the latter is called garbage."

We can also regain that fresh, undifferentiated "seeing" by allowing our attention to stop focusing on the efficiency we need to get through the day and start noticing that which we would normally discard. Some scientists have postulated that it may be that artists see things flatter, which means they find it much easier to paint three-dimensional images on a two-dimensional plane. This might explain how some of the great artists manage to make things look so true to life and give them such perspective.

RITUAL

Viewing art

This ritual enables you to look at things more mindfully, thereby slowing you down. In our daily lives, our brains are processing tremendous amounts of information and we'd pretty much stall if we paid too much attention to everything we see on our way to work. However, if you do this ritual regularly, you will find that you look at the world with new eyes and begin to appreciate the finer details that go into your experience of the world around you. This enhances our sense of compassion as well as making us appreciate the calming effects of beauty.

PREPARATION

Choose an art gallery and preferably go to it at a time when it isn't too busy.

You will need:

Pen

Rituals journal

INTENTION

I look at the beauty before me and am joyful that it exists.

RITUAL STEPS

1 Find an artwork that catches your eye for some reason. It might be the colours used or the shape or the subject. The

important thing is that it should catch your eye as surely as if you had snagged your coat unwittingly and were pulled back to it.

2 Stand softly in front of the work of art, which means standing as though you are a puppet on a string with the string holding you upright, your knees are not locked and you have no tension in your shoulders.

3 Take three deep cleansing breaths through the nose, slowly and deliberately.

4 State your intention – either the example above or devise your own.

5 Relax your body, including your eyes. Glance at the artwork to begin with and then look in detail. Can you find things you did not notice at first sight? Changes in texture or colour that were not immediately obvious?

6 While in front of the artwork, make a note in your journal of what you see. Really drink in the piece. Don't bother reading the curator's note if the work has one. You are your own curator's note.

7 When you are done, leave the gallery without looking at any other art. The intensity with which you undertake this ritual means that only one piece is truly seen. You will cause yourself to slip out of the mode of ritual if you view more. You can always return for a non-ritualistic visit at another time.

JOURNAL REFLECTIONS

Look back at what you wrote in your journal. How did you feel about the art? How did you emotionally react to it? Reflect on what you felt then and what you feel now. Did it remind you of anything in your own life, either now or in the past? Did you find any aspects of it particularly relaxing, be it the colour or the subject matter? I am not a particularly religious person, but I had a completely transformative experience in front of an idol of the Virgin Mary once – the blue of her gown took me to another place entirely and it was just the most spiritually effecting experience.

RITUALISE IT

Try visiting a gallery once a month to look at a new piece of art. Over time, you will find that you are drawn to a pattern in the art you are attracted to – it may be of a particular time period or even one specific artist. Seek out as much as you can that reflects your taste. You may find that this leads you to new parts of town that will then have other interesting and affecting sights for you. While not everything you view will be relaxing or comforting, note when it is so that you begin to build up a picture of what you find calming and soothing.

DAILY BENEFIT

When I was a child, my parents regularly took me to art galleries. This was mostly because we were poor immigrants and that was free entertainment, but it was also because my parents believed that looking at beautiful things elevates us. Appreciation of art is for everyone. Art affects all of us and if you find it isn't your bag, it may be that you haven't found the art that calls to you yet. When we widen our ideas about what is art and who can enjoy it, we find artistry in the most unexpected of places. For example, a grocer methodically putting out his wares is a performance artist when he creates his displays with love and care. As you get used to appreciating art, you will begin to see the art in the everyday and it will inevitably elevate you and your experience of the world.

CREATING ART

If you have always wanted to create art, but were afraid of being no good at it or were discouraged by someone, now is the time to privately give in to that desire. We are all allowed to enjoy making art, even if we're not making a living out of it. Begin with baby steps and a few colouring pencils and a bit of paper. Open a photographic book you like to an image you admire, then try to recreate that image with your pencils. It doesn't matter if it is "good" or not. Your aim is to create something for yourself and to realise that making art is your right. Not everyone needs to win great art prizes or sell paintings for thousands of pounds in order to be artistic – we can all enjoy making our mark and benefiting from the relaxing feeling of being in the creative zone.

Stop and Stare

"What is this life if, full of care,
We have no time to stand and stare."
W.H. Davies, poet

I have taken liberties with the Welsh poet's verse in his poem *Leisure* and titled this section "stop and stare" rather than "stand and stare". This is because I find the best staring is done when seated. Our Western sensibilities mean we often consider staring to be rude and there are only certain times and places we will accept staring. We teach our children that it is impolite to stare and yet we have so much to gain from really looking.

Robert Macfarlane was prompted to write the beautiful book *The Lost Words*, with artist Jackie Morris, when he read research that found that children were more likely to be able to name Pokémon characters than they were wild animals. Another, somewhat disturbing, study found that children spend less time in the outdoors than prisoners do. Now we could go all in for a nostalgia fest about how children used to be able to play out without the threat of violence or kidnapping, but that is hardly helpful. The truth is that we could theoretically all spend more time outdoors as a family, but our screens and the restrictions we have placed on ourselves stop us.

In truth we don't necessarily have to become camping aficionados, nor do we have to move to a rural location to enjoy nature more. I bet you have several different varieties of tree in your local city neighbourhood – extra points if you can identify them all. And we're not enemies of screens, especially when you can now find apps that will help you identify those trees by scanning a leaf. There is a pleasure in knowing the name of the things around you, but there is also a pleasure in just looking without needing to categorise everything we see.

When it comes to our local area, how much do we really "see"? We may pass by great tourist landmarks without ever going in or walk down roads every day we don't know the name of. Have you ever had to direct a friend from the train station to your house? Without knowing the street names, it can be difficult to do so, but often you walk on autopilot down a route every single day without knowing the name of the path on which you are walking. Tomorrow, as you go about your daily round, take a proper look at the views you see every day. Do you know why the roads are named as they are? My south London neighbourhood was famous for producing lavender for the British soap industry and so you get the word "lavender" in many of the street names. Perhaps yours is named for an old word for "hill", which would explain why you need to puff your way up an incline each day.

Do you have any greenery you haven't noticed? How about moss or weeds poking out of city paving stones? Are there any houses that you especially like? Do you pass a particular person at a specific time in the day? Try giving them a non-creepy smile or nod of hello. One of the best practices I was given when I was feeling depressed was to walk around my neighbourhood and look at the roofs of houses. This technique was developed to counteract depressive thoughts – your body physiology becomes upright thereby "tricking" your brain into thinking you are feeling upbeat and then making it a self-fulfilling prophecy. It is also an amazing practice because you often see things you never would

> "Changing your sightline is one of the easiest ways to change your viewpoint to a fresh one."

otherwise, such as unusual houses and gargoyles on churches. Changing your sightline is one of the easiest ways to change your viewpoint to a fresh one.

RITUAL

Sight "seeing"

This ritual is about looking at people and places more attentively. It will enable you to understand the world around you better and, in seeing the hectic pace of others, recognise that behaviour in yourself. Taking the time to do "nothing" is also very useful in learning how to stay calm in the midst of chaos.

PREPARATION

Find a local coffee shop or bar with a large window looking out onto the street. Ideally pick a place you know fairly well so that you can properly notice any differences between what you usually see and what you see when you make it into a ritual of "seeing". Make sure you have one or two hours for this ritual.

You will need:
Pen
Rituals journal

INTENTION

I see the humanity in all and the beauty in the everyday.

RITUAL STEPS

1 Find a seat in your chosen coffee shop or bar that has a clear view of the street outside.

2 Buy a drink and make sure you are sitting comfortably. Place your journal and pen in front of you.

3 Take three deep cleansing breaths to centre yourself.

4 State your intention – either use the example above or devise your own.

5 Sit for an hour or two, just staring out at the world and the people in it. Don't read, look at your phone or listen to music. Be entirely present, by yourself, looking out onto the world around you.

6 Note down any observations and feelings in your journal. What are the main colours you can see? The grey of concrete? Pops of colour in the clothing of passers-by? Which colours soothe your eyes and which make you anxious?

What are the expressions on the faces of those that pass by the window? Do they seem alert or on auto-pilot? Do they seem happy? Sad? Neutral? How does this make you feel? Do you see cars of one particular colour or make more than others? Does the traffic move fast or slow? What are people doing in their cars? Does it look like they are listening to something? Are they tense or relaxed in their expressions? Do you notice anything unusual? A dog breed you rarely see? A mobile mast you never noticed before? Are there any surprises for you in this view?

7 Record all these sights and see if you can find a pattern emerging in terms of the delights and concerns of your local neighbourhood. Note down any feelings that come up for you.

8 When you leave your perch, do take a moment to express gratitude, whether that is with a tip and a thank you to your waiting staff or mentally to a universe that has allowed you to stop for a while to enjoy just staring out at the world.

JOURNAL REFLECTIONS

Look back at what you wrote. Are you surprised by the things you observed? What made you feel most relaxed? What, if anything, did you enjoy and feel positive about? Was there anything that triggered negative or uncomfortable feelings? Reflect on the experience and on how you feel now.

RITUALISE IT

You can do this ritual as often as you like, depending on your schedule and ability to take time out. If you have very little time, do it at least once every three months so you can at least see how the changing seasons affect the sights in your neighbourhood. Is summer more pleasant? Or is winter the time to really see people engage with their surroundings? Note it all in your journal so you can compare each time.

DAILY BENEFIT

If you do this ritual fairly regularly, you will find yourself relating better to the people in your neighbourhood and you will begin to understand that underneath all our differences, we are the same. We all eat, drink, laugh, cry, love, and lose, and all the emotions in between. Nobody is placed higher than any other and, if we're all fundamentally the same, we can't be an enemy to each other. Your sense of connection and compassion with your fellow humans will increase. You will also find some delightful surprises in the local "colour" of your neighbourhood that you can only see if you slow down and do a sight "seeing" ritual.

PHOTOGRAPHY

One way to work with the technology that is prevalent in our lives is to look with a view to taking a photo to share on social media. Instead of just looking for the obvious shots such as selfies in front of flower arches, look for the beauty in dilapidated places and things. In Japan the word *haikyo* means "ruins" and it is also used to describe the practice of visiting abandoned places and photographing their eerie faded splendour. Often where the beauty lies is in seeing nature reclaim its ground from manmade structures, so you have fairgrounds returning to scrubland and palaces swallowed by ivy. These places are also a meditation on the impermanence of life and, as such, can take you away from your everyday troubles.

2

SOUND

"The art of conversation is the art of hearing as well as of being heard."
William Hazlitt, essayist and philosopher

Some sounds will always bring a smile to your face. Not just songs you particularly love, but sounds that have meaning for you personally. It might be the back and forth whoosh of ocean waves or the sound of your baby giggling or early morning birdsong. There are some sounds that are so linked in with a certain place and time in your memory that hearing them again can bring you right back to what you felt at that time.

Now think about the sounds that annoy you. Someone else's tinny headphones on the train. A mosquito in the room. Loud snoring next to you in bed. Perhaps we are willing to mostly put up with these sounds because we enjoy music from our own tinny headphones, we love the sound of the ocean outside that room with the mosquito in it, and we would give anything to hear that whistling snore again after a loved one has passed. The point is context; our thinking about what we hear is as important as the hearing itself.

In couples therapy, one person is often asked to repeat what they heard when listening to their partner. The difference in meaning, intent, and even words that are recalled is often startling. The philosopher Erich Fromm wrote that listening, like the understanding of poetry, is an art. For him, empathy and love are intrinsically bound up in listening to another. For to properly listen to and understand someone – even if you disagree with what they are saying – is to love them. Certainly, relationships improve as couples listen more closely to what each is saying.

Our speech and language development are also closely aligned to our hearing. It is hard to make the sounds we've never heard. In children hearing loss can lead to isolation as they are unable to communicate effectively with their classmates. As such, sound is the sense that is most linked to communication.

SUPER-SENSE

Human hearing is a complex masterpiece – soundwaves
carry through into the ear canal and reach our eardrums.
The vibrations hit intricately calibrated ear bones and
the inner ear, moving the thousands of tiny hair cells and
allowing them to change the vibration into electrical
signals that tell the brain what it is that we are hearing.
It is the work of exceptional engineering and we test
it to its limits daily with music set too loud to play on
our headphones and life in noisy cities. We can hear at
surprisingly high frequencies – on occasion as high as
28kHz (although not as impressively high as the 65kHz
dogs can achieve) and we can hear at lower ones too – as
low as 12kHz under laboratory conditions. Our hearing
deteriorates with age, but it is amazing how little we take
care of a sense that gives us so much joy.

COMMUNICATION AND CONNECTION

Rituals around communication might include making a
regular phone call to a friend or relative. As a young teenager
I drove my parents crazy by constantly being on the phone
to my cousin. Even if we'd spent the whole day together, we
needed an evening debrief just in case a cute boy had been
spotted on the way home. It was vitally important to know if
flirtatious looks had been exchanged. We even spoke in our
own, extremely easy to crack, code and mostly our parents
just accepted it as a normal part of growing up. Now it

may be too much to ask that you call someone every night when, after a whole day of communicating at work, most of us don't want any more chat, but do consider instigating a regular phone call to a loved one – perhaps one who lives abroad – so that you can stay connected through your voice and the sense of hearing.

Music is another sound that gives us connection. I used to be the belly dance correspondent for a dance magazine. I've always been interested in belly dance or *Raqs Sharqi*. The belly dance that we bring to mind in the West is a more cabaret form that was showcased as "Oriental Dance" in 19th-century world fairs, but the roots of the dance lie back in Middle Eastern antiquity. Some have suggested that the gyrating movements were a form of sympathetic magic performed by dancers for women in labour to ease their birth pains. If this is true, then our sexualised idea of the dance is quite far from its roots, but I don't worry too much about its origins and I just like the fun of moving and jiggling your bits. Plus listening to the music has always given me a strong connection to my ancestral roots in the Middle East.

Some songs may make you think about a special person or time in your life, or you may choose to listen to particular music to help connect you to a person or event. We have the notion of "our song" when we think about weddings and first dances. It is a composition that means something because it may well have been playing the first time we declared our love for one another. The sound is linked in with memories and is special because of the memories it evokes rather than the collection of notes and lyrics within it.

Whispering, at 30 decibels rather than the 60 of normal conversation, is another type of communication. There are conventions that we are familiar with in the West, such as whispering at funerals and in churches. Then there are more esoteric uses for whispering such as the rituals of the whisperer-healers (*Szeptucha*) of Belarus and Poland, who use whispered prayers to channel the grace of God. And, while we might not consider whispering in libraries to be a ritual, I pity the fool who risks the high priestess, aka librarian's, wrath with loud talking or laughter.

Almost half of people over the age of seventy-five lose some of their hearing, but that is not the great tragedy of old age. It is that we are listened to less and less as we grow older. Our stories are considered repetitive and our long experience is dismissed as boring. If you do no other ritual in this section, do remember to be kind to anyone you know who is elderly. Who cares if you've heard that story before? The compassion with which you listen to it for the umpteenth time will make it fresh and new. If you are elderly yourself, remember to also listen to the young – they *do* know they're born and they may have interesting opinions to which you can add your own experience, but only after you have properly heard theirs.

THE BENEFITS OF SOUND RITUALS

Almost all religious traditions have an element of sound in their rituals because they know how a pleasing sound can transport you to another state of being. The rituals that follow will connect you to active listening, which can bring you into alignment with sounds that soothe and transport the mind to calming scenarios. As well as trying the specific rituals given here, pay close attention to what your ears are telling you about your life and how you are experiencing it.

SOUND TIPS

- Take as good care of your ears and hearing as you do your eyes or teeth. Book a regular hearing test once you're a bit more advanced in years and do consider pleasant treatments such as Hopi ear candling, in which a tube of waxed paper is inserted into your ear and burned at the top, creating a warm, calming sensation in your ear.
- As much as possible, avoid being exposed to angry, discordant sounds such as loud "shock jockey" DJs or actors yelling in TV dramas. While we do need to hear anger expressed sometimes, if you are already in search of calming rituals, take a break from any unnecessary conflict in your entertainment and media choices.
- Assuming that you don't have ear problems, when taking a bath, consider sinking down so that your ears are covered in the warm water. It can be very relaxing to hear sounds through the medium of water. Just remember to towel your ears properly later so you get all the water out.

Mindful listening

"Ritual isn't about doing a routine mindlessly. It's a way of building something good into your life, so that you don't forget what's important. Done mindfully, a ritual can remind you to be conscious. Done mindlessly, a ritual is meaningless."
Leo Babauta, author and Zen teacher

Pause for a minute and think about what you can hear right now. I can hear the TV ... an episode of a TV quiz. I can hear me yelling out the answers that I know (regrettably all incorrect). I can hear the rain at the window. I can hear my fingers typing on a keyboard. The TV is drowning out most sounds, but, every once in a while, I can hear the wind from the open window rustling the leaves of the large weeping fig I have in the bedroom. The other day I almost jumped out of my skin when I heard one of the leaves falling down the length of the tree, hitting the other leaves. It sounded for all the world as if there was someone here, brushing past the tree.

Your senses can trick you and frighten you if you're not aware of how they work and how the brain fills in gaps, occasionally incorrectly and scarily. When you begin to listen mindfully to what is all around you, fear leaves you and wonder begins to take its place. This is because, with attention, we begin to understand the world around us and what we're hearing.

Funnily enough, when I watch subtitled foreign films or TV shows, I sometimes ask for the volume to be turned up if a character is mumbling and I can't hear what they're saying. Of course, I don't understand a word so it may seem strange to ask to hear better what I can't understand, but I think there is a method behind this madness. We don't just "hear" words, we hear intonation, stresses, and personality in voices. That has nothing to do with the factual meaning of words: those are clues you get that are in addition to the actual words spoken and their meanings.

There is a fascinating sound collection at the British Library in London which contains early spoken word recordings, English dialects from around the world and local histories told in the voices of the people connected to those areas. The huge diversity of what has been recorded is staggering, with the voices of people aged from five to 107. One of the sets in the collection is the Millennium Memory Bank, which is 640 half-hour radio documentaries recorded in the final weeks of the millennium. It is an apt title because our memories and our histories are in our voices. The most authentic reproductions of historical time periods are when the accents of the actors match the area it is set in. The BBC produced a drama series based on Flora Thompson's trilogy *Lark Rise to Candleford* and the best bit about it was that most of the actors spoke in the Oxfordshire accent that you would expect for where and when the story is set.

A few years back, we went to Leeds in the north of England to attend the wedding of two dear friends, Jen and Patrick. It was one of the best and most memorable weddings I have ever attended. Quite apart from the normal fun that you get at a wedding, they had another treat up their sleeves. The venue was Thwaite Watermill, a museum that still has a functioning watermill. In between arrival drinks and the wedding breakfast, guests could walk through the museum, seeing how this Victorian mill used to work and speaking to museum workers dressed in the outfits of the time and doing the jobs that would have been done then. As the wheels still turn, you could also hear the sound of the engineering and the water feeding the mill. It was an amazing, industrial "whomph-whomph" that really brought home the power of the industrial

"When you begin to listen mindfully to what is all around you, fear leaves you and wonder begins to take its place."

revolution. Afterwards we walked down the peaceful canal and listened to the birds and the sound of boats chugging along the water. It was an absolute treat for all the senses, but particularly for the ears.

RITUAL

Sound walk

This is a walking meditation ritual. Go on a "sound walk" – a walk in which the sounds you hear are as important as the sights you see. This mindful approach to a walk helps you become aware of the sounds that you hear each day and allows you to form a memory of feeling attentive, relaxed, and aware when you hear that sound. Over time, you should find that you begin to listen out for the sound cues that then take you back to this walk of quiet contemplation.

The absolute best time to do this walk is on a mid-week day off. I know it sounds like a big ask, but try to do it at the same time as you would if you were going to work. I know, I know, I sound like a horrible person for suggesting you get out of bed on a day off at the same time as you would for your normal commute, but the benefits afterwards will appeal and you can get back to bed after the walk.

PREPARATION

You will need:
A recording device or mobile phone (optional)

INTENTION

I hear the sounds that make me feel held and secure in my world.

RITUAL STEPS

1 Take three deep cleansing breaths in and out through your nose. As you do this, also try to concentrate on the sound of your breathing.

2 State your intention – either use the example above or devise your own.

3 If you find it hard to pay attention to sounds when there are visual stimuli accosting you, you have my sympathies. I am also more visual than aural. You can, however, begin by paying attention to something small like the sound of your footsteps. Then pay attention to other things in layers. The traffic? Birdsong? Other people? Dogs? Children?

4 Do the sounds you hear match what you see and smell? Can you find where the smell of fried onions is coming from? Can you hear a man frying them on a griddle in that food van? The metallic tang of utensils on the cooking surface? If you hear something you particularly like the sound of – say, church bells or the sound of a stream – take out your phone or recorder, if you're using one, and record a clip of it to listen back to later. You don't have to do this if you'd rather not interrupt your enjoyment of your walk.

5 Walk for as long as you are still enjoying finding new sounds. When you're home, you may find that you hear the sound of the kettle boiling more keenly than you did before you went on your sound walk.

JOURNAL REFLECTIONS

Make a note of the sounds you particularly liked on your sound walk ritual. Why did you like a particular sound? Did it remind you of anything? I find the sound of the wind blowing through trees reminds me of childhood camping trips and it immediately makes me feel like I'm in the fresh air, even if I'm walking down a dirty, noisy sidewalk. I focus in on that sound and remember the associations I have with it. What sounds are like that for you? It doesn't have to be what you heard on your sound walk ritual in order to be recorded in your journal.

RITUALISE IT

This is a ritual that you can pretty much do daily, but it is good to do on days where you have enough time to walk as slowly as you like. If you can't do it daily, aim to do it at least once a week.

DAILY BENEFIT

You will find that your sense of sound improves and the associations you have with calming sounds increases, so that you can be transported to a state of relaxation simply through hearing a particular sound on your daily walk. It will be different for everyone.

"I find the sound of the wind blowing through trees reminds me of childhood camping trips and it immediately makes me feel like I'm in the fresh air ..."

NEW SOUND EXPERIENCES

Have you heard the saying 'A change is as good as a rest'? Sometimes we need to hear new things to bring our minds out of habitual hearing and invigorate them to better understand the new – we will then feel relaxed when returning to the familiar. Ask a friend who doesn't share your taste in music to recommend an album that they consider to be one of their absolute favourites. Take time out to listen to it properly and without judgement. You may find you simply can't get through the whole album as it sounds like nails on a chalkboard to you, or you may find yourself expanding your horizons of what you enjoy listening to – the point of this practice isn't the end result, but the mindful listening. Suspending your critical judgement allows you to become a better listener and that will help you throughout your life (even if you'd struggle to listen to any more of that racket!).

While many people may not like the sound of a car door slamming, perhaps it reminds you of childhood holidays when that sound was the start of everyone bundling into the car. You can take yourself to that pleasant memory every time you hear that sound. Keep it as personal to you as possible.

Find your rhythm

"We use rituals in our Moon Circle in order to set the evening apart as a sacred space. We use it to re-centre ourselves, to allow crashing thoughts to melt away. Like music and art, rituals can open our hearts to new possibilities. They allow us to see with a fresh clarity, and bring us to a space of liminality."

Lucy Aitkenread, *Moon Circle: Rediscover intuition, wildness and sisterhood*

In ancient Greece, music was used to cure disorders of the mind. In modernity, we have discovered that soundwaves can reduce blood pressure and enhance mood. I personally am an oddity in that I am not that bothered about music. It is such a universal, human impulse that it seems heretical to say it out loud. I do enjoy folk music and some world music. I do have favourite songs – big nod to Ms Dolly Parton and her magnum opus *Jolene*. I enjoyed the songs at my wedding and handfasting, but I don't share my husband's obsessive daily trawl through musical avenues. I don't go to the gigs he goes to regularly. I don't watch the music documentaries he considers must-sees. I don't play musical instruments. However, a while back, I "birthed" a drum. I know, I know, it sounds like something unspeakable that nurses in A&E departments relate in hushed tones, but that is the phrase for it. When I used to edit magazines about alternative spirituality, one of the subjects we often covered was shamanism. Shamanism is the spiritual belief that we can travel between worlds and meet with helping allies and guides. You don't need to believe in shamanic practices to "birth" a drum and you can even just call it making one, but of course I believe wholeheartedly and so was up for birthing whatever the shamanic teachers, Phil and Lynne Cowley Jones, told me to.

The first time I saw Phil and Lynne, I immediately warmed to them. There is something very compassionate and loving about them. Quite apart from the love they obviously have for each other, they do seem to be on a mission to help people heal themselves. We drove past a beautiful meadow and stopped at a low-lying field with sheep in it and a big yurt on one side. A stream ran at the bottom of the field and it was surrounded by woodland. We went inside the yurt and Phil cranked up the wood-burner making it quickly warm and cosy. The smell of the burning logs was also heavenly and felt like a scent of times gone by.

We began with a healing. With Lynne drumming, I stood in the centre of the yurt as Phil called in our ancestors and guides to bless our undertaking. I had my eyes closed and it was a really strange sensation as it felt as though there were many people around me and, after a time, I had no idea where Phil was, even though I did know he was "smudging" me at times. Smudging (see page 71) is the practice of burning herb bundles and using the smoke created to clear the energy of the person being smudged.

The yurt became a magical place where the smell of incense, the touch of sheepskins on the floor, and the sound of the drumming kept the mundane at bay. All my senses felt tingly and heightened. After this healing, Phil handed me the frame for my drum, a tactile and beautiful wild cherrywood hoop. This was the "bones" of my drum. I was to sand it down and while doing so Phil said my energies would begin to merge with those of the drum that I was helping to create. After I had sanded it, Phil handed me a pot of ochre he had prepared.

The red natural dye represents the blood of the drum and I was to stain the hoop with it. Phil explained that I could either make symbols or patterns or I could just smear it on where I wanted. It was entirely up to me. I dabbed my fingerprints around the inside of the hoop at regular intervals and then covered the whole lot with the ochre. It was a wonderfully messy and enjoyable process. When we're children our parents stop us getting mucky and then when we're adults we do the same, but I found there was something cathartic about getting in there with red dye all over my hands and under my fingernails. The smell was earthy and the coolness of the liquid was in contrast to the warmth from the heater.

The deerskin that would form the skin of the drum was laid out in front of me. There is a herd up in Scotland that the skins come from, and the actual process of tanning the hide and getting it ready for use is done by Phil and Lynne. Lynne explained that it might sound like a strange thing for her to do as a vegetarian, but she honours the sacrifice the deer has made by ensuring she is ever-mindful of where the drum skins come from. Also, there is a belief that the spirit of the animal lives on in the drum.

We then did a ceremony of welcoming in the spirit of the deer and asking for its blessing in using the skin that was before me. This was the most effecting part of the day for me. As Phil sang at the door of the yurt, I imagined a powerful stag running towards me. I could see a sheep in the field beyond and, as I watched, a lamb trotted up to it and began feeding. It felt like a powerful reminder of what it means to birth someone – the nurturing you are obliged to do. As someone who has never wanted to have children, it put me in mind of the other ways in which we nurture and are nurtured in our turn. The practical part of putting holes at regular intervals around the pliable, wet skin came next and then the lacing up with synthetic sinew – the vocal cords of the drum. Working with your hands to make the drum yourself is something very intimate and the feel of skin might make you feel a bit odd, but this is a real reminder of the living creature that it is made from. Lynne then created the right amount of tension for the drum.

We then went on a woodland walk to find a stick for the beater. I saw a fallen ash tree and I cut a small branch from it, then whittled its end and sanded it down. Phil then made it into a beater for me. The rituals done during this workshop were deeply affecting and the end result was a drum that, when played, connected me to that wonderful feeling I had in that field when making it.

RITUAL

Meeting your spirit guide

This ritual expands on the visualisation meditation we did earlier (see page 24). It uses the principles of shamanism to enable you to feel protected and connected in everyday life. You have allies and guides that help you and, even if you don't believe in anything supernatural, your own subconscious invisibly helps or hinders you throughout your life so it can help with connecting to that aspect of yourself too.

PREPARATION
If you can find a CD of shamanic drumming for journeying, listen to see where the different stages of the visualisation begin and end. Alternatively, find any calming music that helps you to

feel mentally transported to another realm. Make sure you can play the music in the room where you plan to do your ritual.

You will need:
CD of calming music or shamanic drumming

INTENTION
I journey to meet the guide who helps me stay calm and focused in my daily life.

RITUAL STEPS

1 Put on the music you will be using for this ritual.

2 Breathe three times in and out through your nose, remembering to focus on the sound of your breath.

3 Then lie down on your bed and relax as completely as you can. You may find that clenching and releasing each muscle group may help.

4 State the intention given above or use an intention of your own if you prefer.

5 Close your eyes and listen to the drumming or the music you are playing. Imagine that each note or drumbeat is sat on top of a line that is vibrating with the sound.

6 Imagine yourself following that line forward in time with the music until you meet someone. This someone may be a person or an animal or even just a shape.

7 Ask the entity its name and listen for the answer. Don't worry if none comes.

8 If your mind wanders to other thoughts, don't rebuke yourself, just bring your attention back gently to the music or drumbeat that is resting on the line.

9 Then, as the music finishes, follow the line back to your starting point and wiggle your fingers and toes to wake yourself up.

10 Open your eyes, but raise yourself up slowly and take a few
   moments to just rest on your bed if you need to.

JOURNAL REFLECTIONS

Reflect on how you felt during and after the ritual. What
feelings did it bring up for you? Make a note of what your
"spirit guide" looked like. If you were answered with a name,
note it down. If not, try doodling in your journal until a
name occurs to you. You may find it is an unusual name.
Research the name or word given and write down anything
you find out in your journal.

RITUALISE IT

You need only find this particular spirit guide once, but you
can use this same ritual to deepen your communication with
the guide and to ask for answers to anything that may be
troubling you. Note any answers or insights down in your
journal, so you can look back later and see how well your
guide advised you on the situation. Did you listen to that
inner voice or ignore it?

DAILY BENEFIT

We all love the idea of being under special protection and
we all are. Even if you don't believe in spirit guides, the
different parts of your awareness look after you all the time,
often without you being conscious of it. As you deepen your
connection with this wiser part of yourself, try to see what
insights it can give you to the problems you encounter. Most
of all, as you go about your daily round, try to remember
the calm feeling the music or drumming gave you during the
ritual. You can return to that feeling whenever you like in
your head.

MAKING MUSIC

If you're particularly musical, there is nothing quite so wonderful as making your own music. There is a very calming genre of music called drone music that often uses field recordings to create ambient sound compositions. When you go on your sound walk ritual (see pages 46–49) see if you can record some inspiring sounds to use in your music-making.

Your voice

"The telling and hearing of stories is a bonding ritual that breaks through illusions of separateness and activates a deep sense of our collective interdependence."
Annette Simmons, *The Story Factor: Inspiration, Influence, and Persuasion through the Art of Storytelling*

Are you as scared as I would be on reading the title of this section? I have a morbid fear of singing – karaoke is an activity I do not participate in. I have met sound healers who insist that anyone can sing, that it is everyone's birthright. They might change their minds if they heard my caterwauling.

Singing is often traditionally at the heart of our annual rituals, from hymns on a Sunday to carols at Christmas. We are expected to sing (and know) the national anthem at times of patriotic display and countrywide ritual. At the very least we should be able to hum along. Voices joining together in chorus is one of the most primal ways of connecting with our community and choirs have been found to facilitate social bonding and help people feel less isolated. It seems that the job of creating a pleasing sound together melds our sense of self to others, making the world seem a much less lonely place.

As I said, I can't sing for toffee but thankfully I do have a soothing speaking voice, even if I do say so myself. I have been asked to do radio presentations and voiceovers. We each have a unique voice that is gifted to us in different ways, sometimes singing, sometimes speaking, and sometimes mimicry. However, fear often keeps it stuck in our throats. Have you ever noticed that sometimes the cleverest people in a meeting are not the loudest ones? The most powerful voices are those that know when to speak and what to say. Overcoming anxiety and speaking up for yourself is one of the most important skills you will ever develop.

Films and TV shows are rife with examples of people practising important speeches, such as wedding proposals and job interviews, in the mirror as a dry run before the actual event. This is not a bad idea at all as you will start to become familiar with your own voice, its undulation and depth. One of the best ways to work with your voice is to read stories out loud. You don't just have to do that with children. One of the nicest experiences I have ever had was my husband reading to me when I had a serious eye infection and was unable to read for myself.

True storytelling, however, is an incredible art and worldwide storytellers and raconteurs are still celebrated for their ability to hold our attention. As a child I recall one magical week when we had a very mysterious supply teacher covering some of our lessons. Instead of paying any attention to the lesson plans left by the teachers he was covering, he decided to tell us ghost stories. Some of those stories still haunt me – but in a good way. I wish I could remember his name since he was the teacher who inspired me to become a writer and tell my own stories. I do remember our drama teacher being livid when he got back that nothing he had wanted us to cover had been done. Since he was one of my favourite teachers, I tried to explain how magical the alternative lessons had been, but I fear my enthusiasm was salt in his wounds.

The griots of Ghana were storytellers of great repute and a drum or rattle would be played to alert people to the fact that a story was about to be told. From tales of Anansi the spider and his interactions with all the other animals in the jungle to fables of African kings, queens, gods, and goddesses, the storyteller had a whole treasure chest in his memory to dig into and delight his listeners.

The difficulty of remembering great tales was brought home to me earlier this year. For years I had been saying that I wanted to try doing a stand-up routine. Like I said, I know I have a good speaking voice, but I had also noticed that when I was giving quite "straight" presentations, such as lectures or guided meditations, my natural inclination was to joke around a bit. I liked the feeling of making others laugh with no more than my words and a meaningful look. So I kept up the fantasy that I could be a great comedian. I have a friend who is an actual comedian, having done training and stand-up in several cities around the world. As a journalist, I had spent a night shadowing the brilliant Canadian comedian Russell Peters and so I thought – with all that osmosis – I knew the backstory of how comedy is put together. You write a show. You memorise it. You present it. Job done. Ha! Not so easy. Eventually I got sick of myself saying that I wanted to do stand-up so in March this year, I got myself a life coach and I put doing a stand-up show down as a goal to fulfil. Then I called my friend who owns a bar that hosts a regular comedy night and asked to be put on the bill. I didn't really plan it very well as I only gave myself two weeks to put together a routine and memorise it. The hour before, I was frantically pacing trying to remember what was on my index cards.

When I got there, the venue was brightly lit (as one of the other comedians that night said on stage, it was the only place he'd played at where the audience were as well lit as the performers). Alas this meant that I could see everyone looking at me, in particular a young man at the front with his arms folded and an expression that said, 'Well, make me laugh then.' It was awful. My throat was dry, my heart was pounding. I remembered most of the routine, but I was so nervous that I ran through it way, way too fast. I had some lovely comments from the other comedians afterwards saying that it was really great for a first time, as some of them had properly frozen and tanked at their first appearance. And I had even had a couple of kind laughs. It was not as appalling as I thought it was – or indeed it had felt it was. However, I no longer held the fantasy that I could be a comedian. I understood fully and completely how tough it is and how the truly great ones make it look so damn easy. In writing the routine for that evening, I realised how important it is to write

"It seems that the job of creating a pleasing sound together melds our sense of self to others, making the world seem a much less lonely place."

down what you want to say first. For some reason, it sticks better to see and read the written word before you make it your own and say it without thinking too much about it. There is an alchemy to it in that it starts as a story you would tell a friend in the pub, gets written down with all the pauses and unnecessary digressions taken out, and then read out again as the best version of itself. It is a good exercise to do in processing some of our childhood stories too. Bear in mind that the stories we tell ourselves about our lives — like the words from one partner in couples therapy (see page 37) — are not necessarily the way others see it or indeed the absolute truth. This doesn't make you a liar; it just means that you have a perspective on a tale and it may not be the only or the most complete interpretation of it.

RITUAL

Storytelling

We all tell stories, about ourselves and about those around us. Some of the stories are truer than others, but all of them come from the prism of our own experiences and can never be fully objectively true. This ritual puts aside the need for truth and instead allows you to tell the best story, the one that best serves you and your happiness.

PREPARATION

Take your journal and settle yourself down somewhere for an hour or two when you won't be disturbed. Do this in a room where there is no one else about and where you won't be overheard. The more private it is, the better you will be able to express yourself.

You will need:
Pen
Rituals journal

INTENTION

I speak the truth that gives me most pleasure and joy.

RITUAL STEPS

1 Take three cleansing breaths in and out through the nose, in order to move yourself into the space of ritual.

2 State your intention as given above or devise your own.

3 Then take up your pen and write a story from your childhood. It doesn't need to be great literature and you can use a different name to get some distance in the tale if you're not comfortable writing it as straight autobiography. It can be about your first day at school or something less momentous, such as your favourite hobby when you were growing up.

4 Then read it aloud to yourself. Try to listen the way an objective person would. Does this story ring true? Do you like this story? Is the main character sympathetic or have you written it so that you give a harsh appraisal of yourself and your actions?

5   If you find that you don't like the story because it makes you feel sad or uncomfortable, try rewriting it in the way you would like it to have happened.

6   Then read it out aloud to yourself again. The energy of this second, better, reading is what you can take with you into your day.

JOURNAL REFLECTIONS

Write down how this exercise made you feel. Would you be happy to repeat it with other stories you tell yourself about yourself? Which are the stories you never want to write? Could you reframe them in a way that would make you happy? Remember you are now in a position of distance from the past. It can no longer hurt you – as long as you don't let it. This ritual can powerfully enable you to take back ownership of the story and also give you the outcome you would have wanted instead of the one you got.

RITUALISE IT

Do this ritual as often as you feel comfortable. It is probably the most challenging one in this book as we often tell ourselves terrible tales about ourselves – we highlight our failures and ignore our victories. Be gentle and kind with yourself and only do as much as you feel right for you at this time.

DAILY BENEFIT

Hearing your story told out loud in your voice and making it the tale you want to tell about yourself is powerfully transformative. You can finally forgive others and yourself and move forward. Many of us are mired in the past and it isn't always a comfortable place to be. Using the power of your own voice, step into the present and make it the best experience you can.

CAMPFIRE TALES

Memorise a good ghost story, perhaps nothing too scary if you plan to share it with young children around. The next time you are in front of a fire, tell it to the folks around. Do all the voices and try to get them to jump at the right places. Gathering around a fire-burner in the garden is brilliant for this, as it means you have a fire on tap whenever the weather permits. Otherwise, camping is a real pleasure (especially if you get a decent airbed) and nothing beats the joyous ritual of roasting marshmallows and telling stories in hushed tones to each other. It is transcendent.

3

SMELL

"For the sense of smell, almost more than any other, has the power to recall memories and it is a pity that we use it so little."
Rachel Carson, marine biologist and author of *Silent Spring*

Freshly brewed coffee, baked bread or cookies, freshly laundered bed sheets, newly cut grass, vanilla – these are just some examples of scents that are almost universally enjoyed. Our sense of smell is so closely mixed in with our memories and emotions that we can use the smells we find most pleasant very effectively in rituals to induce a feeling of calm. Studies have shown that even the idea that a pleasant smell is in the room will lift the mood and perceptions of the people present. The actual smell being there is doubly effective. Weirdly enough, research shows that we will even decide that people are better-looking if they smell good – definitely a handy finding for the perfume trade.

GOOD AND BAD SMELLS

Favourite smells are very individual and not everyone is on board with those that are traditionally considered

SUPER-SENSE

The sense of smell is the sense most closely aligned to memory and emotions. When we smell something, olfactory neurons at the top of the nose send an impulse to the brain along the olfactory nerve. This reaches the part of the brain called the olfactory bulb, which then interprets the signal and gives information to the limbic system about what that smell means. The limbic system, thought to be one of the oldest and most primitive parts of the brain, is a complex one that plays a vital role in behaviour, mood, emotions, and the storing of memories.

good. Many years ago, I became obsessed with burning frankincense resin after smelling it at shamanic workshops. To me, it smelt like sacred space and transported me to a place of healing and sanctuary. When my mother visited, she wrinkled up her nose and insisted I open the windows as for her this scent was closely aligned to death. Where she grew up, frankincense was burned in funeral parlours and at death rites, so for her it had negative associations – the smell was closely aligned with sadness and fear of losing loved ones.

A friend of mine could not stand the usually very relaxing smell of lavender because it reminded her of the lavender-scented floor cleaner her mother used whenever she'd been sick as a child. Her associations with lavender were of vomit and sickness, not relaxation and beautiful gardens. Mine are of the stunning lavender fields in bloom in the county of Surrey where I live. Each summer I try to get over to see them and walk the length of the rows, held in a bubble of heady aroma. These examples highlight how extremely personal the sense of smell is. It is important to select your own calming scents because what smells gloriously lovely to you may bring back distressing memories for others. Also be aware of how the scents you choose might adversely affect someone else in your household.

I live alone with my husband so there is only one other person to consider when I'm introducing new smells into our home. Luckily, we mostly agree on what are pleasant and unpleasant. There have been unfortunate missteps resulting in an expensive new home fragrance being donated to the goodwill store because it was deemed to be "eeeurgh".

Stinky feet, dirty toilets, and stale cigarette smoke are universally reviled (no, smoker at the back, it isn't a lovely smell if it is still lingering in your upholstery three days later), but we soon get used to certain smells if we are exposed to them enough. I grew up in a smoking household and one of my schoolfriends would upset me by saying she could smell the smoke on my clothes. I couldn't smell a thing and thought she was just being her usual catty self. Her redemption came years later when my husband quit smoking and took up vaping. At the time, I visited my parents at their home where my dad still smoked. My mother gave me a new top she had bought for me, which had been left in a bag in the living room. When I got home from my parents, I sniffed the top and realised I couldn't wear it without washing it first as it stank of cigarette smoke. I hadn't been able to smell it at my parents' house as that was my childhood home and my nose was used to the smoky atmosphere. At our home, newly de-smoke-fragranced by an ex-smoker husband, the smell was all too apparent.

Your sense of smell will be blind to certain things, so do be aware of that when going about your daily business. If you suspect that you have bad breath or your deodorant isn't doing its work, ask someone you trust to tell you the truth. These things can be embarrassing, but it is far better to walk out in the world knowing that you have made yourself as pleasant to others as possible than just bumbling along not quite understanding why you're clearing a room. Don't, however, offer that gem of advice without it having been asked of you – nothing ends a friendship quicker than being told you stink. Just ask the friend who got it in the neck for her honesty about my stinky smoky clothes.

You also need to be aware that your body chemistry changes over time and so the perfume that smelt absolutely divine on you at age twenty will not necessarily smell the same at age forty or sixty. I was told by a perfumier that people should go fragrance shopping at least every couple of years so they can find out if a scent still suits them. He advised using unscented soap in your shower on the day of the shopping trip and not to go if you had a cold. Rather than spraying perfume on those little cards (they only give you the top notes since the perfume develops on the skin), spray a small amount on your wrist and let it dry without rubbing it. Then sniff it. See how you like it. Try a different scent on the other wrist, but don't try any more perfumes than that. You can then walk about on your shopping trip and try smelling the perfumes again in a hour. This is when your nose has got used to them and the richer base notes will be coming through.

THE BENEFITS OF SMELL RITUALS

The rituals in this chapter are likely to most affect you since our sense of smell is so keenly attuned to our memories and our emotions. Really enjoy these experiences as there is no greater everyday luxury than scent and we can use it daily to bring about a sense of calm. As well as trying the specific rituals given here, pay close attention to what your sense of smell is telling you about your life and how you are experiencing it.

SMELL TIPS

- Keep a small bottle of essential oil or an essence stick at your place of work. Then, if the day gets a bit too much for you, take a sniff of the scent in order to remind you of more calming times.
- Swap out your scents by season. You know how cinnamon and cloves immediately remind you of winter and holiday celebrations? Well, see if you can find scents for each and

every season and use them liberally, so you can access the pleasures of that season whenever you smell those fragrances.

- If your partner has bought a scent that reminds you of a bad experience, be honest and ask if you can replace the fragrance with another that they like but that is inoffensive to you.

Smudging

"The goal of smudging is to make a place clear of lingering energy that is different from what you may be intending for that space. You want to prepare the space for ceremony, the way you would clean your house, cook, and decorate when your family comes for a holiday. We are welcoming Great Spirit, angels, and ancestors to come and share clean space with us as well."

Grandmother Wapajea Walks on Water, healer and singer

'Have you been smoking weed?' My husband had just walked in from work, sniffed the air of our flat, and shared his suspicions. I had not been smoking marijuana, which is still very much illegal in the UK. I had been burning white sage as part of a ceremony to clear our home after I had given it a spring clean. It was not the first time I had experienced the two smells being mistaken for each other.

A couple of years back, the mind, body, spirit magazine I worked at had an anniversary party at a pub in a nice part of town. My boss, the managing director, had walked in, pulled me to one side, and insisted that he could smell someone smoking weed. I assured him that it was the white sage being burned by our ad sales manager at the back of the room to create the right atmosphere. My boss had previously managed some of the most popular music magazines in the country and so his exposure to rock star debauchery and drugs had been extensive (though he says he never inhaled) and he insisted he knew the difference. He did not.

Smells are part of the indefinable qualities that make your house into your home. As a first-generation immigrant, the child of political refugees, I have had conflicting ideas about which country I belong in, but never about the homes I lived in. The feeling you get when you open the door to your home is sacrosanct. It is homecoming in the sense that the smell and atmosphere engulf you on entry. That might be the smell of curry as it was in my childhood home or the smell of nice Jo Malone candles as it was in my bachelorette pad. Now it is the combined smell of my husband's vaping juices, my cut flowers, our home cooking, and all the other minute chemical markers that tell me that this is where I belong. Among them is the trace of smudging smoke (not weed).

Smudging originates in Native American ceremonies, but it has been embraced by those who are into alternative spirituality as a way to clear out negative energies. It has become something of a cliché, with many examples in film and TV of kooky characters using it as a prop for commentary on more "square" characters. In the brilliant TV show *Grace and Frankie* there is a good example of this – Frankie's hippie character is shown smudging Grace's more straight-laced waspish one. It is the ritual that is most likely to draw raised eyebrows from family and friends – and certainly I draw a lot of fire whenever I smudge our house. My brazen attitude is to try to smudge the person doing the mocking since you can smudge both people and areas. I hope you are also able to take any jocular comments in your stride and smudge with the best of them.

RITUAL

Smudging

This is a great ritual not just for clearing the energy of a home, but also for reminding you of the presence of sacred wonder in your life. This can be easy to forget when children are screaming the house down, the dinner's burning in the oven, and your partner has helpfully left the toolbox right where you can stub your toe. The truth is we are all just one burning herb bundle away from calm, so get yourself smudging to create that peace.

PREPARATION
Begin by thoroughly cleaning your home, or at least the room you wish to smudge. This is important because it begins the process of cleansing and shows that you are serious about the ceremony.

You will need:
Pre-made smudging sticks or make your own by tying dried sage, rosemary, and lavender together in a bundle with string. Fireproof bowl or ashtray

INTENTION
I create a happy, clean home, which nourishes and supports me and my family.

RITUAL STEPS

1 Take three deep breaths in and out through your nose, to centre yourself.

2 Then state your intention. You can use the example given above or make up your own, as long as it is present and positive.

3 Light the end of the smudging stick and blow on the end to get smoking embers. You can then pass the smoke clockwise around the room that you are working in. Do try to get under furniture as well as up high so that the smoke permeates.

4 Once you have finished, press the end down on the bowl to stub the stick out and leave it in a safe place to use again until it is burnt down. Never leave a lit smudge stick unattended, even if it is in a fireproof bowl. Stub it out.

JOURNAL REFLECTIONS

Reflect on how you felt during and after the ritual. Make a note of how your room (or home if you did the whole house) felt after the smudging. What memories or feelings did the smell of the smoke evoke in you? Did you wish it always smelt like that or did it feel odd, like someone else's house?

RITUALISE IT

I smudge my home weekly, but I know some people only do it once a year after a spring clean. This is entirely personal so decide what feels right for you and

"The truth is we are all just one burning herb bundle away from calm, so get yourself smudging to create that peace."

do it with that regularity. If you found that you didn't like it, you can instead engage in mindful cleaning using products that smell good to you.

DAILY BENEFIT

The benefits of having a clean home are many as the energy flows better and you feel calmer being in an organised space. Smudging shifts something in that energy, something indefinable that can only be experienced rather than explained. Try it yourself and see how that shift benefits you.

PEOPLE SMUDGING

If you find a person willing to smudge you, it feels fantastic and can immediately make you feel more relaxed. Here is how it is done.

1   Stand in front of the person with your eyes closed.
2   Starting at your feet, they should take the smouldering smudge stick (see above) and pass the smoke over your entire body counter-clockwise. They should move up the left-hand side of your body slowly, over your head, and down the other side. They should finish at your feet, having done three passes, then stub out the stick (see above).
3   Ensure you have a glass of water to hand and sit still and relax and enjoy the fragrance for a few minutes.

Essential oils

"I invite you to drink in the divine nectar of aromatic love and let it penetrate you in the deepest, most profound ways. Trust that the oils are working side-by-side to heal, regenerate, and teach you. The more you use them, the more they'll reveal their secrets to you."

Elana Millman, *Aromatherapy for Sensual Living: Essential Oils for the Ecstatic Soul*

The first time I smelt an essential oil is one of the clearest memories of my life. I was about ten years old and my parents had taken us to the Mind, Body, Spirit Festival in London. Years later, when I was presenting on stage at the festival, I remembered my childhood visits and felt such a sense of continuity and connection with my tribe. No matter how much my dear, dear friends take the mick out of my "hippie" tendencies, I love that I have an unbroken line going back generations to alternative forms of spirituality and healing. It is why I can remember sharply my father holding a small brown bottle under my nose and saying, 'Smell that.' It was jasmine. It smelt like night-time walks in the country of my birth – heady, exotic, and warm. My sister and I had been bought crystals and beads and so should have been happy with our haul that day, but I kept going back to the small bottle. Eventually my dad gave it to me, probably because he thought I would end up spilling half of it if I kept sneaking into his study to get another hit of jasmine scent. He bought me a small oil burner, showed me how to use it, and told me to never, ever leave it unattended.

I started a ritual of burning it ten minutes before bedtime and then blowing out the tealight in the burner and laying in the dark with the scent of night-blossoming jasmine throughout the bedroom I shared with my sister. It remains a favourite smell for both me and her.

Using essential oils in the bedroom is one of the best ways to start a journey into scent and bring calm to your everyday life. It will turn the room in which you sleep into a scented haven. It is also handy to know that studies have shown that certain smells can help you sleep better. When CBD oil manufacturers create vials of the oil for people to use on their skin before bed, they add calm-inducing lovely scents to the mix. They are not required to do that for the CBD oil to work, but add them because the smells are wonderfully relaxing.

Sleep specialist Joy Richards says that the smell of lavender has resulted in a 20% 'better than average' increase in the quality of sleep in some studies. This is because it has been shown to slow down the nervous system. She says, 'Sprinkling a few drops of lavender oil underneath your pillow, or on a piece of tissue, has shown to increase slow-wave sleep. Slow-wave sleep is your "deep sleep" where your heart rate slows down and your muscles relax, resulting in you feeling far more refreshed and energetic the following morning.'

I once visited Meadows aromatherapy company at their headquarters in an old oasthouse. The smells were absolutely amazing. With several hundred essential oils stored on site and in the development areas, it was all aroma and loveliness, but I realised that the staff working there could no longer smell how wonderful it was. A lady in the warehouse told me that it is lovely coming in to work first thing in the morning as you can smell the scents, and she did use some of the oils at home, but that, yes, during the day your nose stops giving you that hit of aroma.

You can use essential oils in several ways. Try mixing a couple of drops of your chosen oil into a base oil like almond or coconut and get a helpful loved one to massage you with it (see page 121). Or if your loved ones are being actively unhelpful, try a face steaming using a relaxing oil such as lavender or bergamot. Put a few drops into a bowl of hot water, cover the bowl with a towel, then put your head under the towel, and inhale the heavenly scent deeply. The steam from the hot water will also help open your pores, so you also get a lovely facial. If that is too intense a heat for you, add the oils to a warm bath instead. Just be sure to take care when stepping out of the bath as it may well be slippery afterwards. You can also buy face oils to rub into your skin at bedtime.

> "Using essential oils in the bedroom is one of the best ways to start a journey into scent and bring calm to your everyday life."

RITUAL

Relaxed bedtime

You probably already have a bedtime ritual, consisting of brushing your teeth, washing your face, and setting your alarm. If you have difficulty relaxing and falling asleep, you can use scent to heighten your bedtime ritual to one where you fall asleep in a sensual scented space.

PREPARATION

Ensure that your bedroom is not too hot and change your bedsheets weekly so you have fresh-smelling sheets against your skin. Remove any gadgets from your bedroom or at least turn them to silent.

You will need:
Essential oils
Oil burner

INTENTION

I sleep well and my dreams give me insight into my life.

RITUAL STEPS

1 Light a tealight under an oil burner next to your bed and burn a couple of drops of a relaxing essential oil such as bergamot or lavender. Let the air fill with the scent for a few minutes.
2 Take three deep breaths while lying in your bed, after you've turned out the lights and are ready to sleep.
3 Say your intention aloud, either the example above or your own devised one.
4 Blow out the tealight under the oil burner.
5 Notice things objectively like the weight of your duvet on your skin and the feel of your gentle breath.
6 Let any thoughts come and go without judgement.

JOURNAL REFLECTIONS

In the morning, record how you felt during the ritual and whether you felt it made you calmer and sleepier. Record any dreams you had. Are there any insights for you there? Did you focus on a particular issue that you wanted guidance on? How did your dream make you feel?

RITUALISE IT

Do this ritual daily and try to retire to your bedroom at the same time each night. This will begin to allow your brain to start communicating more clearly with your subconscious, enabling you to access information about how you feel about different situations while you sleep and giving you more meaningful dreams.

A NOTE ON ESSENTIAL OILS

If you are pregnant, always check whether it is safe to use an essential oil. These are powerful products that can help you immensely, but they are strong and so need to be used with care.

DAILY BENEFIT

The scent you smell during this ritual will become a marker for rest and relaxation. Then when you smell it at any other time, you will feel deeply relaxed and rested. You can then use this ritual for times such as travel overseas or when your sleep patterns are disrupted. The smell becomes a way to tap into your body's own sense of calm.

Conscious smell

"Control of consciousness determines the quality of life."
Mihaly Csikszentmihalyi, *Flow: The Psychology of Optimal Experience*

There is an advert on TV for an air freshener that uses the phrase "nose-blind" to describe the phenomenon I spoke of earlier, when you get used to a scent and can no longer smell it. We often go through life "nose-blind" until we come across a smell that we're not expecting, such as a smell to alert us to a burning dinner or a gas leak. A scent that reminds us of an old boyfriend. An unpleasant stench that tells us something nearby has died or gone very, very off. However, we have a "scent scape" underneath all those big, bold smells that is there if we want to activate it.

Close your eyes and put this book under your nose – what can you smell? The ink-on-paper smell that books exude? Does the book smell differently near the spine than at the ends? Can you smell the glue in the binding? Open it up and bury your nose in the pages. Did you notice that smell earlier when you were reading? Probably not because it was faint, so faint that your brain decided it wasn't a smell worth flagging up. Put the book down and smell your hands. Do they smell of the soap from when you last washed your hands or do they now smell of the paper, ink, and glue of the book you were just holding? Either way, you are likely to have smelt more this time than you usually do when you hold your hands up to your face. This is because you have consciously decided to smell things on the basis of the instructions here.

We often take our sense of smell for granted and only mourn it when it is not there. It is quite intensely connected to our sense of taste and so it is harder to taste food if you have a cold and a blocked nose. I spent a lot of time in my youth hanging out with chefs as I was editing a restaurant magazine. They couldn't imagine anything worse for their profession than losing their sense of smell. It was as important – if not more – than the sense of taste because scent molecules will often predict what it is you think you're tasting.

> "We often take our sense of smell for granted and only mourn it when it is not there."

When a foodie friend lost his sense of smell, it was tragic on many different levels, but mostly because he lost interest in his great passion, being no longer able to taste as well as he once could.

You did a "sound walk" on page 46. This time I'd like you to take a "scent walk". You can cheat and go somewhere known for spectacular scents, such as a physic garden where each herb will give off a heady scent, or you could do a simple walk through your local neighbourhood. Your aim is to find out what your area smells like and to undertake the walk with conscious intent. Keep a nose out for any particularly pleasant smells.

RITUAL

Scent walk

A scent walk ritual puts you in touch with the smells that form part of your daily life. When you become conscious of what you're smelling, you appreciate the variety that is presented to your senses daily and can enjoy finding the scents that particularly move you.

PREPARATION

Try to do this ritual at a time that you're not rushing, preferably in your local area rather than somewhere new, so that you can properly smell where you spend most of your time. Don't do it if you have a cold and can't smell as well as usual. Wait until you feel better.

You will need:
Tissue infused with a pleasant-smelling essential oil

INTENTION

I am grateful for my sense of smell and all the delights it affords me.

RITUAL STEPS

1 Take three deep cleansing breaths, in and out through your nose, before you start your walking ritual.
2 State the intention for your walk, either the one above or one of your own devising.
3 Walk slowly, discreetly smelling the air without any over-the-top sniffing. As long as you are breathing in and out through

your nose, you should be able to catch a sense of what you're smelling. If you find that you can't discern any smells, sniff the essential oil-infused tissue to awaken your sense of smell and then see if you can smell any contrasting scents once you have removed the tissue from your nose.

4 Don't be disappointed if your nose is greeted with mainly unpleasant smells. Petrol fumes, dog mess, and rubbish might not make for the most enjoyable scent walk, but they are good indications that your sense is working well and you should be grateful for it. Aim, if you can, to find some green space, no matter how small, so that you can enjoy the fresh smell of grass and flowers.

JOURNAL REFLECTIONS

Reflect on how you felt during and after the ritual. Note if the main smells in the area where you live are pleasant or unpleasant. When I lived in Manchester, I was located quite near to "the curry mile" of Rusholme and each and every day the air was scented with the delicious smell of curry. Now that I live right next to a common in south London, it is the smell of heather and cowslip that scents the air. Are you surprised by anything you smelt?

RITUALISE IT

You can do this ritual once every season to check how the smells you discern change over the course of the year. Even the air smells different as the weather changes, so see how detailed your sense of smell gets when you really pay attention to what you're smelling.

DAILY BENEFIT

Keeping your sense of smell in tip-top condition is only possible if you keep using it consciously and with intention. By doing this walking ritual every few months, you remind yourself that this is a sense you want to develop and enjoy. You can also use the suggestion in the box below to discover which smells you find most alluring and ensure those form part of your daily sensory pleasure.

DAILY "SCENTUAL" JOY

Make a note of five smells that you particularly like – not perfumes or colognes, but ones you might come across in daily life. Ensure that you smell one of your favourite smells daily, whether that is in a cup of tea or through burning essential oils. This will contribute to your daily happiness in a way that you wouldn't believe. Here are mine to inspire you and start you thinking.

1   Bergamot
2   Earl Grey tea
3   Freshly cut grass
4   Limes
5   Narcissus

4

TASTE

"Everyone eats and drinks,
but few appreciate taste."
Confucius

If you're anything like me, you really look forward to mealtimes as a pause in the day to give in to joy. From the endorphin rush of a really spicy curry to the delight of a cheese-laden pizza, tasting food can be a real pleasure. On the downside, it is our sense of taste, and the pleasure we get from it, that often drives us to overeat certain foods and to use it to "comfort" ourselves. If something tastes great or provides a good mouthfeel, then we will want more of it. We do, of course, have an obesity crisis in the West, but this isn't helped by the fact that as a society we bombard people with faddy diets and insist that they should obsess over what they eat. We all saw where obsession over chocolate got the priest in Joanne Harris's *Chocolat*.

Taste is also deeply embedded in the sense of smell (see page 65), so, while something might taste alright, if it smells "off" most people would be averse to eating it. Our sense of taste has

SUPER-SENSE

When we eat or drink something, chemicals are created in our mouths that then bind with taste-receptor cells, activating them to send a message to sensory neurons. These neurons send a nerve impulse to the brain that lets us know what we're eating. The different-shaped taste molecules that enter our system when we eat different food and drinks let us know if they are sweet, salty, sour, bitter, or umami. That last one is a sort of savoury taste that has only recently been discovered and is still a little bit contentious depending on who you ask.

developed to help us survive so we can tell what is good to eat and what is bad. When we crave something, it is often related to what is happening in our blood chemistry, so it is a powerful tool used by the body to ensure we get all the nutrients we need.

PERSONAL TASTE

We don't all develop our sense of taste to the same level, but some people have it to a phenomenal degree. I was editor at the Quality Food Awards, where top food and drink consultants, chefs, and foodies would gather together to judge hundreds of products. You could see how incredible their palates were in the notes they produced while judging.

When I visited some of the development kitchens at UK and Irish supermarkets, I saw how much of a science it was to develop recipes that could be broken down and reformulated so that they could be made in bulk under factory conditions. It is a fascinating industry, but it is a million miles away from how most of us cook or even think about food and drink, focusing as it must on preserving products for transport and longer shelf life. Better education about where our food and drink come from, and growing concern over health, has meant that we now eat far less processed food and drink. While this is laudable in some respects, it can begin to make us repetitive in what we eat. We can get into a food rut when we focus too much on restrictive diets.

We probably have more daily rituals around taste than we do any of the other senses. Most families have habitual ways of eating, whether that is sitting with their food on their laps in front of the TV or being seated around the table together. We are told that it is beneficial to eat one meal together and it seems intuitively correct that if we put our gadgets down and really focus on our families at mealtimes – or at least at one mealtime – it will make us feel valued and improve our connection to each other. However, it doesn't mean that you are not connected to your family if you don't do this. Families can exhibit togetherness in a variety of different ways and we aren't required to follow the cultural norms of others to feel good about our choices. For example, in some parts of the world people consider it very rude to be observed when eating and so have their meals in private.

Nourishment is vital to our survival, but taste is a very personal thing. However, many people want to tell us precisely what we should eat. Religions have restrictions based around food and drink, and I have often been shocked by how the obsessive chefs I have known have insisted that not only should people try food they are not fond of, but that they should enjoy it. Many of them have also grumbled viciously about vegans. I have always found this behaviour really odd since what we put in our mouths has to be one of the most personal, intimate choices. Don't let anyone bully you into eating what you don't want and don't let anyone force you into food rituals of society's making. If you hate turkey, don't have it at Christmas. Can't stand champagne? Celebrate with what you like drinking instead.

"If you hate turkey, don't have it at Christmas. Can't stand champagne? Celebrate with what you like drinking instead."

You may have taken a sharp intake of breath there and that's because our seasonal rituals around food and drink are so deeply embedded in our cultural and personal lives. Each Christmas my mum-in-law will eat a dry turkey crown (and I'm sorry but, no, turkey is *never* not dry – you can baste it till the cows come home at which point you can abandon it and have beef instead). We always have a different meat at Christmas if she's not spending the holidays with us. Traditions that make you unhappy should be abandoned.

Also, be careful about what you eat and when. A friend found she could no longer eat blueberry pie, formerly one of her favourites, after it was served at her boyfriend's funeral. Blueberry pie, like a song or a scent, is linked forever in her mind with grief at losing her beloved.

THE BENEFITS OF TASTE RITUALS

Food and drink are so primary that we don't even notice how much they occupy our lives. You probably already have many rituals based around taste, but the ones in this chapter will remind you what it is to truly taste a thing – to focus on its flavour and texture and how it makes you feel. This can be life-affirming stuff and we don't call it "comfort food" without good reason. Learning to eat differently and with more intent can turn every mealtime into a more calming, relaxing experience. As well as trying the specific rituals given here, pay close attention to what your tastebuds are telling you about your life and how you are experiencing it.

TASTE TIPS
- List out the foods that always tick your "comfort food" boxes and stock up on them.
- Unless there is a strong health reason not to, give up on diets for a while – especially if you're an obsessive or habitual dieter. Discover what freedom to eat whatever you want feels like. Trust yourself to choose nourishing foods.

- Remember to eat slowly and chew properly. This is a part of mindful eating, but it is as good for your body as it is for your mind – it aids digestion and lets you know when you are full.

Tea

"I say let the world go to hell, but I should always have my tea."
Fyodor Dostoyevsky, novelist

Assuming you enjoy drinking tea, there isn't much that isn't made better by a nice cuppa. From the very ritualistic tea ceremonies of Japan to the daily cuppa of most Brits, tea is vital to the well-being of many. In Britain every terrible thing that happens is punctuated with a cup of tea, as if it will mend everything from a broken heart to sudden grief. It may not be a cure-all, but the ritual of making and drinking tea comforts us in so many ways.

When my grandfather in Pakistan died, we were in the UK. Some bright spark put an obituary in the newspaper with the details of our house where prayers would be taking place. It is the duty of every Muslim to condole at the death of another Muslim, if they hear of it. It is considered a blessing to have many people at your funeral and/or prayer meeting. So, in our tiny terraced house in Willesden Green, London, we had hundreds of people coming and going, reading verses of the Quran. These folks simply needed to be fed and served tea. My mother and a local caterer friend set up a pot the size of a small human in our back garden and cooked from morning to night, and I was on tea duty.

Over several days, before and after the date of the prayer meet, visitors came to condole. I started making tea on autopilot. A number of days later, one of my dad's friends popped round to take him out. However, within the five seconds of him stepping into the living room, I popped in like a tea ninja with a tray of tea. My dad gave me a big hug and told me that my tea duties were now at an end. The terrible sadness of losing my granddad had been mitigated somewhat by the practical job of making tea for whoever crossed our threshold.

Nobody knows the exact origins of tea-drinking, but some say it was discovered in 2737 BC by the Chinese Emperor Shen Nung. A servant was boiling some water for the Emperor's supper when a few leaves from a nearby tree flew into the pot. The Emperor, being an adventurous sort, decided to partake of the liquid and loved it and the rest, as the legend goes, is history.

There are literally countless teas in the world. Every estate produces a different tea on a different day. Tea expert and blender, Alex Probyn told me, 'There are ten to fifteen leaf grades and about 8,000 estates (if you count smallholdings too) in India alone so you can imagine, it's a huge number of different teas.' Alex uses around 400 different blends in his work.

Tea increases blood flow to all parts of the body and stimulates the brain. It is also a good source of manganese, copper, zinc, and amino acids – all of which you need in a healthy body. Polyphenols in tea have antioxidant properties that diminish free radicals in cells that can cause cancer. Tea has also been shown to have a beneficial effect on rheumatoid arthritis in some study groups. All this amounts to tea being pretty darn good for you.

Some researchers at City University in the UK found that putting the kettle on and having a single cup of tea after a stressful event reduced the level of anxiety in participants by up to 4%. However, the leader of this study, Dr Malcolm Cross, thought it may have had a psychological basis in "Britishness" and the shared cultural idea of "putting the kettle on" being a soothing act.

Interestingly certain brands sell better in different parts of the UK as factors like water quality will affect how the tea looks and tastes. The mineral levels in water cause it to be "hard" or "soft" and this can affect the quality of the cup of tea you make. In the UK we are fairly married to the idea of putting milk in our tea, but this is not the case in most other European countries.

When Alex blends tea for a particular person, he will take all of this into account as well as looking at the person's age, background, what tastes they like, how adventurous they are, and other aspects of their demographic. He'll also ask for any anecdotes that allow him to get a better idea of the person he is blending for. Then he puts his creativity to work and brings forth a blend that is made to each individual's requirements. 'I like to think that there's a perfect blend for everyone,' explains Alex, 'but you can have different blends for different moods and effects. Certain teas like rose and chamomile are soporific and can help people sleep, but you'd need to drink a lot of it to actually induce sleep. Raspberry leaves are a natural relaxant and lemongrass is a natural stimulant so you can get natural highs and lows from tea.'

While you will have heard of black and green teas, the new demand from tea connoisseurs is for white tea – the leaves are picked pre-dawn before the sun has changed

"It may not be a cure-all, but the ritual of making and drinking tea comforts us in so many ways."

the colour of the bud. This special tea is high in antioxidants and is a more delicate variety of tea. As more and more people travel and seek new culinary experiences, the future looks bright for the rare tea market. At auction some of the rarest teas can sell for thousands of pounds. However, you need not spend a fortune on your daily calming cup – just experiment with different varieties till you find one that really makes you smile in the morning. It is not trite to also say that if you are in the midst of a panic or starting to feel overwhelmed with stress, get up and make a cup of tea. As the water boils, you can take some steadying breaths, remember that life doesn't have to be this way and that it is only your thoughts that are causing you to suffer, and then pour the water for a refreshing and revitalising cup of tea.

RITUAL

Tea-making

Joel Biroco, a Zen tea master, taught me this ritual for tea-making, which is precise, detailed, and unyielding. I have adapted it to incorporate my own ways to stimulate the senses and enjoy the process even more. This isn't a ritual for every time you have a cup of tea. It is a special one for when you can really give a bit of care and attention to the process.

Then, when you make a "normal" cuppa, you can draw on the feelings that this more luxurious ritual gave you.

PREPARATION

You will need:
Loose-leaf tea (my favourites are Earl Grey and Jasmine)
Teapot
Tea cosy
Tea strainer
Cup and saucer or Chinese teacup (a mug just won't do!)

INTENTION

I nourish my body and soul with this aromatic tea.

RITUAL STEPS

1. State your intention, either out loud or in your mind. You can use the example above or your own.
2. Boil fresh water.
3. Pour a little of the boiling water into your teapot, swirl a couple of times, and pour out.
4. Add a teaspoon of tea per person plus one extra to the pot.
5. Fill the teapot with boiling water and stir once.
6. Put the lid on and cover with a tea cosy.
7. Take three deep cleansing breaths, in and out through your nose, as you wait for the tea to brew. Allow the tea to infuse for three to five minutes, depending on how strong you like it.
8. Stir once more.
9. Replace the lid and pour the tea, using a strainer to catch the stray tea leaves. Put the cosy back on the pot to keep the tea warm.

10 Add milk and sugar to taste. Don't add milk to green tea and
   note that you can re-infuse green tea a few times by topping
   it up with hot water.

11 Slowly and mindfully sip your tea, taking care to smell the
   aroma of the tea you have chosen.

JOURNAL REFLECTIONS

We all need to take proper breaks in life – the tea is optional.
Reflect on whether you take enough pauses in your own
life. Make a note of times when you have properly paused.
Have you ever taken a sabbatical? Maybe an impromptu day
off in which you did nothing but mooch around the house?
Have you ever been forced to take a pause due to ill health
or unfortunate circumstances? Check in with yourself – did
it make you scared of pausing? Decide what level of "tea
break" you are willing to have in your life – one long holiday
each year or a few long weekends? Diarise those pauses and
treat them as sacrosanct.

RITUALISE IT

Do this ritual once a week, perhaps on a Sunday when you
have more time. You can invite friends to come and take tea
with you, but ensure you're all on the same page in terms of
treating it as a shared ritual. It won't feel the same if you're
all giggling and not taking the ritual seriously. The ritual of
tea-taking is much more about looking inward and seeking to
create a calm memory that you can then call on later.

DAILY BENEFIT

If you take care over this weekly tea ritual, the calming
pleasure it brings will infuse all of your ordinary tea breaks.
If you chose a particular scented tea, such as Earl Grey, for

your ritual buy tea bags in that flavour and your brain will take you back to the calm process of the longer tea ritual whenever you pop that bag in a mug.

FORAGING FOR TEA INGREDIENTS

The author and foraging guide Adele Nozedar suggests that a great way to connect with the scents around you is to forage for your tea ingredients. She recommends the following: "Gather a couple each of nettle and dandelion leaves, and a few strands of goosegrass (also known as cleavers, this is the sticky stuff that kids throw at each other) per person; steep in a pot of boiled water for approximately 3–5 minutes."

Adele explained that all these wild, fresh leaves are full of antioxidants and are energisers, so will make for a great pick-me-up tea. Nettle boosts the immune system and cleanses the kidneys, and dandelion is a diuretic; its bitter leaves are a boost for the digestive system, helping to break down fats. Finally, cleavers, as well as having a fresh flavour, very much like pea shoots, are a tonic for the blood.

Fruits

"Fruit... it's just God showing off. 'Look at all the colours I know!'"
Dylan Moran, comedian

Dylan Moran is my favourite comedian in the whole wide world and, as you know, I am slightly obsessed with comedy. There are two reasons why he's the best in the world. The first is *Black Books*, a cult TV show – if you haven't seen yet, please go find it and watch it from start to finish. You will not regret it. The second reason is that his stand-up comedy is always truthful. If you look at all the different fruits of the world, the myriad colours *do* look like someone has been showing off.

The fruits of my childhood – mango, guava, plums – can transport me back to my grandparents' house in an instant. The smell, the taste, the juice running down my elbow – a delight for all the senses. I also remember very clearly specific fruity experiences, such as the ripe papaya I was served in Australia for breakfast each day, or the fragrant lychee I had at the end of a meal in a Thai restaurant. Often fruits are linked in with childhood memories because that is when we get bombarded with fruit. When your impulse is to shove every sweet thing in your mouth, your parents attempt to head you off at the pass by making it fruit instead of candy or chocolate. Easy-peel satsumas and bananas are the fruits of our youth. As we grow older, our tastes change and of course there's no one to restrict us from those unhealthier options. Who ever picked a fruit platter over a chocolate fondant for dessert?

However, the sheer variety of different fruits out there in the world mean we should not ignore this bounty. There are at least 1,600 varieties of banana in the world and Kew Gardens puts the total number of plant species – and therefore fruits – at around 390,900, although only around 2,000 of them are suitable for human consumption. Given that most of us probably can't even name 100 fruits, let alone a thousand, we have plenty of scope for experimentation.

It can be good to check out your local farmers' market to get varieties that you're unlikely to see in supermarkets since they are not commercially grown. You can also ask folks at your local allotment to see if they will give or sell you their extra harvest so that you can again try different varieties of fruit and veg.

In the Victorian era, it became very fashionable to grow pineapples as a way to exhibit your wealth. Since they didn't grow very easily in the British climate, serving a pineapple at your grand dinner showed that you had access to a greenhouse, and could afford to heat it and employ a gardener to look after the plant. Only the very rich could enjoy such a luxury. It would be quite astounding to time travellers from that era to discover that now absolutely anyone can have a whole pineapple just by popping down to their local shop.

Some climate change activists warn that if we don't wake up soon to the destruction we have visited on the planet, our everyday luxuries such as oranges and bananas will no longer be as readily available. It is often the case that we don't miss some things until they are gone. So now is the time to start appreciating these small miracles and getting your "five a day".

RITUAL

Savouring a strawberry

This ritual elevates the eating of a strawberry to another level, but if you dislike this fruit or it is out of season, you can pick another one and simply apply the same principles.

PREPARATION

This ritual is best done in summer when strawberries are in season. You can pick or buy any type of strawberry and you only need one.

You will need:
One strawberry

INTENTION

I am grateful for the opportunity to really appreciate this single fruit.

RITUAL STEPS

1 If you have several strawberries to hand, pick the most appealing one from your punnet.

2 Place it in the palm of your hand and take a really good look at it. Is it a small woodland variety or one of the massive ones you often get in supermarkets? Is it even in colour? What is the colour telling you about its state of ripeness?

3 Take three deep cleansing breaths, in and out through your nose, and then state your intention either using the example above or worded in your own way, as long as it is present and positive.

4 Take a sniff of the aroma of the strawberry. Is it strong or delicate?

5 Take the smallest bite of the fruit, letting that distinctive strawberry taste spread across your mouth. Is it juicy? Is the flesh tender or firm?

6 Finish the strawberry by continuing to take small bites that spread the flavour throughout your mouth.

7   When you have finished, don't rush off into your day; be still a while and appreciate the wonder of the universe that created such a miracle as the humble strawberry.

JOURNAL REFLECTIONS

First reflect on the ritual and any feelings it brought up for you about food and the way you eat. How was it different to eat the strawberry in this mindful way rather than grabbing it and eating it on the go? Think about your most transformative food experiences. Write down every little detail that you can remember. If it was cockles on the beach, describe the whole experience from the sounds and sights of the sea, to the tang of vinegar on the cockles, to what you drank with them. If it was your favourite chocolate as a child, what was it that appealed? The taste, certainly, but was it the melting texture too? The mouthfeel, as we food writers call it? Write down as many wonderful food experiences as you can in your journal and see if you can recreate one or two of those experiences over the coming month.

RITUALISE IT

Try a week of eating one fruit this mindfully, perhaps at your breakfast table if you have time before work. Alternatively, do it as you come in from work if the mornings are far too rushed for a ritual. Try to capture that sense of being completely present – only you and the strawberry exist for that particular moment in time!

DAILY BENEFIT

We often eat without thinking, but a really conscious, ritualistic way of eating brings you home to the wonder of the experience. We are often blessed with ripe fruits and vegetables in season, but can sometimes wolf things down without much thought. This process of paying more attention to taste will awaken you to the gifts of the harvest. You will never look at these simple fruits the same way again once you have taken this much care over eating just one of them.

FRUIT VARIETIES

See how many different fruits you can enjoy in a single week and you get extra points if it is something you have never tried before. Try to eat seasonally as that is when each fruit tastes best. A fun approach is to eat a fruit each day that starts with that day's letter – so a mango on Monday, a tangerine on Tuesday, a watermelon on Wednesday, a tayberry on Thursday, a fig on Friday, a strawberry on Saturday, and a sugar apple on Sunday. Alternatively, pick a letter a week and only have fruits beginning with that letter. Restricting yourself in this way immediately makes you want to have things "off programme", so make a note of what you're missing. If you're on apples and you fancy an orange, either have it then and there or add it to your shopping list for next week. Have fun with it. Be playful with your week and try your best to get as many odd and unusual tastes in there. You will begin to understand how much diversity there is in our wonderful world. You will also find that the scent and taste of some fruits calm you down immediately because of the memories linked to it. Ensure you make a mental (or indeed actual) note of those and keep them in your emergency kit of what to have when you're feeling particularly stressed.

Mindful eating

*"One cannot think well, love well, sleep well, if one
has not dined well."*
Virginia Woolf, *A Room of One's Own*

I was once invited to eat at Dans Le Noir, a London
restaurant in which you eat in the pitch dark served by
blind waiting staff. You choose what you want to eat from
the menu in the lit reception and then you are led into the
blacked-out dining room by staff. I had chosen a chicken dish
served with some form of potato. Eating it was ridiculously
difficult and I soon forewent my cutlery to eat with my hands
(not great when it is a dish with gravy). I also found I did not
enjoy my meal as much and could not distinctly taste what I
was eating. It may well have been that the mindfulness with
which our hosts wanted us to approach the experience was
missing in the hilarity that ensued by feeling for your pal's
face to work out where they were sitting. It also turned out
that they seated people next to strangers on tables of four so
I was sitting next to someone I did not know.

The idea is that your sense of taste is enhanced, but this
didn't happen for me. The whole experience felt like it should
have been better than it was and I didn't repeat it. I am also
hampered by the fact that I am a food bolter. I eat quickly
(sometimes so quickly I give myself hiccups) and then I run
off to enjoy the rest of my day. This isn't because I don't enjoy
food and only see it as fuel – I absolutely love it, but I am also
completely ravenous by the time I want to eat and I am not at
all mindful about it.

One of my friends eats so slowly that meals with him are
exhausting. By the time that I would normally be asking

for the bill, he has just started his entrée. However, he does properly chew his food, know the different components of what he is eating, and makes interesting judgements on whether he likes it or not. I am a much more that was "yum" or "yuck" type of eater.

We could all do with being a bit more mindful of what we eat. Not just in terms of the actual food we put in our mouths, but also in terms of how it gets on our plates. Some of our farming methods leave a lot to be desired and, whether we acknowledge it or not, the guilt we feel about eating highly processed, cheap food can impact our psyches. The best way to get mindful about eating is to look at your food chain. Is what you're eating ethically produced? Does it taste fresh? Are you happy giving it to loved ones?

Our budgets can often restrict us in what we can eat, but learning to cook can help counteract that. When we were going through a particularly poor period in our lives, the recipes of Jack Monroe saved us. Cooking on a budget is possible, but mindful cooking, whether on a budget or not, is absolute salvation. You start to think about food not as another thing to pay for, but as an affordable pleasure. Jack's penny pizzas made our lives

"We could all do with being a bit more mindful of what we eat. Not just in terms of the actual food we put in our mouths, but also in terms of how it gets on our plates."

better, not just because they were cheap to make but because it was the first time that I had thought about making pizzas from scratch. The sense of achievement you get from home-cooking is quite something else.

RITUAL

Mindful mealtime

You may already have a ritual of setting the table and sitting down to at least one meal with the whole family and if you are religious, you may also say a prayer of thanks before eating. This is a more secular ritual that is also about thanksgiving, but it can be done once a week instead of as an annual celebration.

PREPARATION

This is best done as a shared family ritual – if your family are not up for it, you can still do your part of it mindfully and accept that they are not keen on it. However, do ask them to put down and silence gadgets for the duration of the meal and to sit together. If you don't have a dining table and chairs, put down a picnic rug on the carpet and some cushions and still sit together in a circle so you can see each other's faces.

INTENTION

I appreciate and am grateful for the food I prepare and eat.

You will need:
A recipe you know and love
Ingredients for the recipe
Candle
Table and chairs to sit around (optional)

RITUAL STEPS

1   Prepare your meal. As you cook, think deeply about the meal nourishing you and your family. Think about the blessing of the

farmer who grew the ingredients, the retailer who got it to you, the maker of the implements with which you are cooking.

2   As your pot simmers or you pop your dish in the oven, give gratitude in your heart to all the very many people that have been involved in the making of this meal. Don't forget to include yourself for making something with your own hands to nurture your family.

3   Set the table and place a lit candle in the middle.

4   If your family are willing, join hands and take three deep breaths, in through the nose and out through the nose, together. If they aren't willing, do this yourself.

5   State your intention – either use the example given above or devise your own.

6   Then, in eating the meal, chew each morsel carefully and think about the flavours of what you're enjoying.

7   Look around at the circle of your family and feel the love that you have for them. If you live alone, look down at your hands holding the cutlery and think about how much you love your body and all that it does for you.

8   Take as much time as you can over your meal – afterwards extend the feeling of joy and nourishment by chatting over a cheeseboard or after-dinner digestif.

9   When you leave the table to clear away the dinner dishes, give thanks either verbally or in your mind to the universe for the food you've eaten and the health and happiness of your loved ones.

JOURNAL REFLECTIONS

First reflect on the ritual and any feelings it brought up for you about food and the way you eat. How was it different to eat a meal in this way? Did you feel calmer? Did it help you to enjoy and digest your food? For further reflections, consider what dinner you would most miss if you were stuck on a desert island. Write it down in detail. Make it three courses. This is the good bit – you're not stuck on a desert island! So one night this week, enjoy your absolute favourite meal of all. If nobody else in your family likes it, cook it just for yourself. This act of self-nurture will remind everyone – including yourself – that you are important and worth the extra care.

RITUALISE IT

Ideally all meals would be like this, but it can be hard to gather everyone together, get them to put down their blippety-blips, and get on board with connecting in that lovely way. As such, maybe save this ritual for once a week on a Sunday when everyone is usually together for a family meal anyway.

DAILY BENEFIT

When your child is being stubborn and your partner is being annoying, it can be hard to remember all the very many things we love about them. This ritual will align you to the love you have as your constant baseline. It will remind you to be patient with your loved ones when they are being impossible. It might also teach all of us to slow right down and really savour our food.

TRYING NEW FOODS

Find a recipe you have never made before. It can be for a meal you often enjoy when dining out, but have never made at home. This is important to do every once in a while to avoid getting into a food and drink rut. You can even write out a bunch of recipes on individual slips of paper and pick one out of a hat to try each time you're looking for inspiration.

5

TOUCH

"Touch seems to be as essential as sunlight."
Diane Ackerman, author and poet

Your body's workings are incredible and, as we reach the final part of your five senses, we come to rituals around the most intimate of the senses – touch. The hug of a loved one, the giddy excitement of a first kiss, and the exhilarating sensation of wind on the face are all brought to us through this incredible sense. It is touch that allows us to know where we end and others begin.

When we say we feel "comfortable in our skin", we mean the whole external part of us that we show the world is in alignment to the person within. As children, one of the first things we do when we're upset is avoid the touch of others. Our sense of touch not only tells us how we are feeling about ourselves, but also lets us know if we trust or like someone else.

The first thing that happens when you are born is that you are placed in your mother's arms and that skin-to-skin touch is the first notion of touch outside the womb. No wonder a baby cries so robustly when all this sensory overload kicks in. This first experience of touch is when a bond begins between a mother and child.

For some of us, our next vital bond – that with a partner – starts with a kiss. We all remember the best kisses we've had – the one from the long lusted-after boyfriend who finally goes in for a smooch. Our terrible first ever kiss (practising kissing on the back of your hand as a teenager is never the same as another's lips).

A VITAL ORGAN

Your skin is more than just a medium for sensitive romantic touching; it is the organ that lets you express empathy, love, and care. A counsellor once told me that anyone who has either broken up with a long-term partner or been widowed should go for regular massages. He believed that the thing people often miss the most is someone touching them in a focused, kind way. As humans we need touch to feel connected with those we love. Even if you're from a family that is not very demonstrative, you are likely to want some form of touch, even if it is just a firm handshake in greeting.

SUPER-SENSE

Our sense of touch works by relying on a number of different receptor groups. The first group is in your skin, the largest organ of your body. The skin sends five different types of signal to the brain about what is happening to it. You perceive temperature, pressure, pain, and stretching through your skin and that enables your brain to tell you how to navigate in the world. Your sense of touch also indicates how well your brain is working because it relies on signals from the brain. Often we only become aware that something is wrong because we can no longer feel a certain part of our body or do a simple action such as making a fist with our hand. We rely on our sense of touch for important information. Your skin would alert you to pain if you were to scrape your arm on a wall. It would let you know if someone squeezed your arm to get your attention. If you feel a breeze, your skin can tell you where it is coming from.

My family are, regrettably, very demonstrative and every poor child in the room is engulfed in perfumed hugs. As a child, I remember a friend of my parents visiting us. She was wearing a huge fur coat and I was horrified since I had recently turned vegetarian (fur coats are still anathema to my beliefs, unless you live in a tribal situation in arctic conditions and have no access to synthetic fibres). She scooped me up in a dreadful bear hug, made more bear-like with that awful coat. She then pinched my cheeks and ensured I would tell my mother for years afterwards what a terrible woman she was and how my parents should be ashamed that they put me in contact with her.

That example above says lots about consent and boundaries. Often, out of politeness or cultural norms, we don't think enough about touch and permission. A friend of mine said she would never in a million years tell her child to give anyone a hug or a kiss unless they expressly wanted to. She had been made to hug aunts and uncles and grandparents as a child, and she was not a natural hugger. She felt awkward and didn't like it. She feels that it is a violation of the child's right to decide about their own body if they are made to act in a certain way due to so-called manners or expected ideas of physical affection among family members. There was a great video doing the rounds on social media a few years back of a nursery school teacher who allowed children to choose between a dance, a high-five, a hug, a handshake, or a bow when entering their classroom in the morning. She said she wanted to teach them about physical boundaries and that it is always their choice as to how physical they want to be with someone else.

Children – and dogs for that matter – can often sense sadness in a person and can be surprisingly kind in their reaction. The touch and physical closeness of those we love can make all the difference to how we feel. I remember when I lived at home and had suffered a bad break-up with a boy. I was in bed in the afternoon, miserable under my duvet. First my middle sister turned up and sat at the foot of my bed, telling me things she thought might cheer me up. Five minutes later her five-year-old son and two-year-old daughter joined in, squished on top of me like wolf cubs on the small single bed, which was by now creaking under the weight.

"Our sense of touch not only tells us how we are feeling about ourselves, but also lets us know if we trust or like someone else."

The icing on the cake, however, was when my youngest sister then fetched her house rabbit and set him down on top of me and then also climbed onto the bed. I don't know if you've ever had the experience, but it is very hard to stay miserable with a toddler, an infant, two grown sisters, and a rabbit on top of you. When I asked my small nephew how I could get back to being happy, he replied, with the simple wisdom of youth, 'Eat lots of sugar and move around.' On the whole, not bad advice at all. Our brains give us a reward response when we ingest sugar and fat, which is why we crave ice cream when we're sad. It just makes us feel better.

BENEFITS OF TOUCH RITUALS

Are you "touchy-feely"? Touch is not just about touching another person or yourself – it can be the sensual delight you feel when standing on a soft rug or gently touching a velvety plant leaf. We pat someone's hand when we want to reassure and calm them and you can do the equivalent for yourself by paying attention to what you touch and allowing it to calm and reassure you. You can find ways to incorporate touch into everyday rituals if you remain awake to the possibility of texture being a way to connect with yourself and others. As well as trying the specific rituals given here, pay close attention to what your sense of touch is telling you about your life and how you are experiencing it.

TOUCH TIPS

- Make applying cream or oil to your body after a bath into a ritual by paying close attention to how your muscles and body feels when you massage the lotion into it.
- Don't ignore daily aches and pains – this is your body communicating with you so remember to keep your eyes and ears open and get medical attention when you need it.
- Touch the texture of the clothes you are currently wearing – do they give you pleasure? If not, choose a piece of clothing for texture alone and have a little feel of it whenever you feel you need a little self-hug.

Self-massage

"Self-care is never a selfish act – it is simply good stewardship of the only gift I have, the gift I was put on earth to offer to others."
Parker Palmer, author, educator, and activist

Think about what you instinctively do when your shoulders feel tight or you have an aching neck. You stretch and attempt to massage the site of your pain to relieve the tension and help loosen the muscle. This is just what you do naturally as an embodied creature, but you can also look after your body in a variety of different ways. I have tried a number of ways to massage and heal my own body – perhaps the weirdest of them all was when I was buried alive. Yes, you may well splutter out your coffee. The lady at Lewes council did when I asked for permission to dig my own grave in Sussex woodland for a shamanic burial. However, it was eventually agreed. The burial is primarily done by the person being healed – the idea is that the earth "massages" you when you are in your "grave".

As crazy as it sounds, being buried has been used as a healing and initiatory practice in many cultures for more than 40,000 years. Shamanic healer Ross Heaven said that being "held" by the earth can effect a profound healing on a person, allowing them to overcome trauma and emotional upset as well as having a beneficial effect on physical ailments. It is done overnight and the person emerges re-born the next day at dawn.

The first part of the healing, however, is physically tough-going. You have to dig your own grave as this is part of the process. You also fast from midnight the night before. You are only allowed water and tea or coffee. The grave is kept fairly close to your actual body shape so that you are quite tightly held in place – this is so that the earth makes contact with each part of your body, giving you a full body massage or "hold" without anyone else touching you. The ground was hard and unyielding and my hands blistered with the digging almost immediately. Three hours later, I was still only about a foot and a half down and I needed to be about three feet down. Ross revealed that the digging itself was a meditation and how hard or easy it was could be a sign of what I needed to know too. If that was true then my grave was telling me that my life was really hard and pretty shallow!

Then, with night fast approaching, I put a ground sheet, sleeping bag, and cushion in the hole. I climbed in and thin planks of wood were put down to support the weight of the soil, which were then covered by tarpaulin. I felt completely tucked in, each part of my body making contact with the compacted earth around me. There was a wide gap at the top of the tarpaulin for air but, once it was dark, you couldn't see where that was. Then Ross threw spadefuls of soil over me and I felt the weight of the soil upon me. It was really strange seeing the soil all around me, the different strata of chalk, soil, and granite rock interlaced with termite holes. The smell was of the earth when it rains and it was quite comforting. Then I got an itchy nose and had to wiggle my arm up to get my hand to my face and felt how enclosed I was and the panic of claustrophobia kick in. I had to regulate my breathing and remember that I could come out whenever I wanted. Ross would be right next to me the whole night. I immediately started thinking of urban myths, like some psycho in the woods turning up and killing Ross and then filling in my grave for a lark. I also got as far down in my bag as I could so that any worms couldn't wiggle into my ears. Both these fears were irrational, but felt more real at the time. Every once in a while, I could hear Ross drumming and this always seemed to calm me down.

I couldn't stick to it the whole night and at about midnight (about four hours in), I heard a voice telling me that it was okay to quit. I asked to come out. I then had a brief rest by the campfire before filling in the hole. I had to imagine that I was leaving behind anything I didn't want, like fear or pain, in the hole.

The next day I felt really renewed, but the most dramatic thing I discovered was that it is okay to quit when I'm not enjoying something. Prior to the burial, I would stick to things until the bitter end through some false sense of it being the "right" thing to do. Saying 'no' or 'no more' has been really liberating. So, would I get buried again? No.

"I have tried a number of different ways to massage and heal my own body – perhaps the weirdest of them all was when I was buried alive."

Easier methods of self-healing are massage chairs and physical self-massage of the parts of you that you can reach. Alternatively, find an essential oil or cream that most appeals to your sense of smell and use it in the ritual below.

GREEN FINGERS

You don't have to be buried alive to enable the earth to help in your healing. Gardening is a brilliant way to de-stress. The physical demands of the activity keep you fit and using your hands to re-pot plants and feel the cool earth beneath them is a deeply affecting experience. If you don't have access to a garden, consider getting yourself an indoor plant pot. Ferns are my favourite, but pick whatever appeals to you. Make it a daily ritual to at least say hello to your leafy pal – even if the plant can't hear or answer you, it will enjoy the carbon dioxide you breathe out on it when you speak near it. Name the plant if you're really up for it and make its care part of your weekly rituals of slowing down.

RITUAL

Hands of love

Your hands should be thanked regularly for they do so much for you from holding things to your daily work to enabling you to hold the face of a loved one. As well as being calming, this ritual honours and pampers your hands, allowing you to express your gratitude to them on a daily basis. Keep a lotion or your oils by the sink in your bathroom for ease of daily use. Do take a little time over this one and, as always, build in a little time to gently return to your fast-paced day rather than immediately returning to the daily grind.

PREPARATION

You will need:
Hand cream made by mixing a couple of drops of your favourite essential oil into an almond or coconut oil base
Alternatively, pre-made or shop-bought hand lotion or cream

INTENTION
I honour the hands that enable me to show active love in my world.

RITUAL STEPS
1 Take three deep cleansing breaths in and out through your nose.
2 State your intention, either out loud or in your mind. You can say the one above or create your own if you prefer.

3 Then, using a little of the hand cream, massage one of your hands carefully.
4 Pay attention to every line, every knuckle, every cuticle.
5 Gently squeeze up and down each finger.
6 Massage your palm in circles.
7 Go down to the wrist and encircle it with small massaging movements.
8 Take your time and don't rush through the ritual. As you massage think about all that your hands do for you and express your gratitude through the care with which you massage each one in turn.

JOURNAL REFLECTIONS

Reflect on how this hand massage felt for you. Did it help you relax? What other feelings did it bring up for you? Then draw around your hand on one of the pages of your journal and doodle some patterns on the outline. Look for symbols that mean something special to you. It could be your favourite flower or the name of a loved one hidden in intricate patterns. Brides in the subcontinent often have the name of their husband hidden in their wedding henna so that his finding it in the pattern breaks the ice on their wedding night. After all, what better excuse for hand-holding? You don't have to henna tattoo your pattern onto your actual hands, just having it in your journal and looking at it will remind you of the little symbols of people and things you love.

RITUALISE IT

This is a ritual you can do several times a day, if you wish, because it is so very easy to keep some hand lotion by the wash basin in the bathroom or in your bag. Just do it in line with the ritual above and you will get into the habit every time you have a toilet break.

DAILY BENEFIT

Quite apart from having super-soft hands, you have pressure points on your hands that are activated when you massage them with care. This promotes a sense of calm and allows you to re-enter that state whenever you touch your fingers, even when you're not doing a self-massage ritual.

Massaging loved ones

"Healing begins with an aromatic bath and a daily massage."
Hippocrates

I have had some massage training because I used to review spas for magazines and, as part of that work, I attended a few evening classes to learn about classic Swedish massage. I was fascinated by the different styles of massage and a particular favourite was Lomi Lomi, a Hawaiian practice that does not always include massage, but which has been brought to the UK as a massage therapy. The practitioners I had met doing this massage said that loving care was an absolute requirement in the treatment. You did it from a point of honouring the person receiving the massage.

I wanted to do this myself and so I picked my mother as my first "victim". I very carefully laid out towels on her large bed. I then put a small warming plate with some oils on a side table and I had already properly readied myself by having a short nail manicure (long nails should be banned in anyone performing massage) and wearing a short-sleeved T-shirt and loose yoga pants.

I got my mother to first lie on her front as I massaged the back of her legs, her back and arms, finishing up with her head. I ensured the oils I chose smelt so nice that I didn't want to rush through the whole process. I also thought about all the wonderful things that my mother does for me and I wanted to do the same for her.

When I got her to turn over and I massaged her face and décolletage, she was almost asleep. She still remembers it as one of the best massages she has ever had. Of course, me being horribly fickle, I never went back to my training and haven't given many massages since.

I have always mentally showered blessings on really skilled massage therapists, who shine in comparison to those who are clearly thinking about their to-do list rather than really engaging in the process. Then there are the loud, chatty massage therapists, who can completely ruin the ambiance that has been set by the scent, music, and soft lighting.

If you would like to experiment with treating a loved one to a massage, think about what you like in a massage and commit to doing that for them. The worst thing is when someone massages you for a bit and then decides they're bored or tired. Commit to a full hour so that you leave the other person feeling properly relaxed. Take turns on different days so you both feel properly pampered.

If you hate massages – and there are some odd people who do – then you can also connect with just a snuggle in front of the telly instead. If you're usually very tactile, try to spend a couple of nights not being so and see how it feels. If you're usually very restrained, try being physically affectionate and see if you like it.

RITUAL

Tension release

This is a ritual you can do lying down in bed at any point in the day. Alternatively, if you have a willing partner, have them come in and do this with you and for you. You can take turns with your partner so that you both get to enjoy the calming effects of a soothing massage. This is a bit less stringent than a full massage, but is equally relaxing.

PREPARATION
Close the door to the bedroom if you think you will be interrupted by curious children or cats.

You will need:
Two pillows

INTENTION
I am comfortable and happy in my body.

RITUAL STEPS
1 Take three deep cleansing breaths in and out through your nose.
2 State your intention, either using the one above or devising one that works for you.
3 Place one pillow under your head and the other under your knees.

4 Place your hands on your stomach so you can feel the way your breath makes this rise and fall.

5 Lying very still, do a full scan of your body in your mind. Take your attention to your feet and see how they feel. Do they feel sore? Can you feel a blister from new shoes? Are your arches hurting? What about your ankles?

6 Slowly move up the body, mentally asking each part how it is feeling and whether there is any tension or pressure at those points. Whenever you come across a point of pain or pressure, ask your partner to touch it and soothe it very gently. The healing that comes with light touch is often just as profound as deeper massage.

7 If you're by yourself, you can also soothe the painful area yourself by lightly passing your bare hand over it, acknowledging that it hurts, but also remembering that your body has a miraculous capacity to heal.

8 Once you (or your wonderfully obliging partner) have slowly done the whole of your body, have a nurturing little nap.

JOURNAL REFLECTIONS

Reflect on how it felt to do this ritual. Did you feel calmer for it? What other feelings came up for you? Is there anything you'd do differently next time? Then write an expression of your optimal health and bodily comfort. This means you write how you'd like to feel every day in your own body. If you often have itchy, dry skin, write that you would like to have soft, supple, wonderful-feeling skin. If you have a recurring injury, write an expression that says that you have strength in that area. Really visualise what being ultimately happy in your body feels like. Then note down some steps you can take to begin to make that expression a reality. If you need to get medical assistance, do so. Make your health a priority.

RITUALISE IT

Do this ritual at least once a month. It is a good way to check your body for any changes and to ensure that you are in tip-top condition. Plus it is a wonderful way to connect with your partner, if you are doing the ritual with him or her.

DAILY BENEFIT

You will find that you grow in confidence when you show your body some focused love in this way. It is the principle of loving kindness in action and will always make you feel loved, even if you do it for yourself. As Oscar Wilde said, "To love oneself is the beginning of a lifelong romance" – so get romantic with yourself and the whole world will follow suit.

MASSAGING OTHERS

You may love being massaged yourself, but can think of nothing more tedious than massaging someone else in your turn. Keep an open mind and do it anyway. Your pleasure in giving might surprise you. If you use delicious-smelling oils and take your time and give it your full attention, you will find that you gain as much in the giving as you do in the taking. All of life is give-and-take and the more you give, the more you will get in your turn. Remember that the next time it is your turn to give the massage.

Pressure points

*"Your sacred space is where you can find yourself
again and again."*
Joseph Campbell, Professor of Literature

Acupressure is a practice that is part of Traditional
Chinese Medicine and works on the principle that there
are meridians of energy running up and down your body.
The points identified on the body are in places you wouldn't
expect to be connected with the organs and processes they
are. For true acupressure, it is worth going to a qualified
practitioner, but you can practise stimulating points in your
body through a number of different practices. For example,
yoga is a great way to get in touch with your body. One of
the main yoga postures that most Westerners will be familiar
with is the sun salutation, but instead of just doing the
posture in class, you can take the idea of greeting the sun
into your everyday life.

Stand facing direct sunlight, close your eyes (don't ever
look straight into the sun), and breathe in through your nose.
Put your arms loosely at your side, ideally with your palms
facing the sun. Let the light and warmth permeate through
your skin and on your face. Notice the red hue of your
eyelids. Breathe in the scents of summer if that is the season
you find yourself in. Listen to the sounds around you, from
lawnmowers to buzzing bees. Irrespective of your spiritual
beliefs, give thanks for the vitality we receive from the sun.
It doesn't have to be to a personal god, it can be to life itself
for existing. Don't rush opening your eyes and going about
your day. These moments you take to enjoy the sunshine

and the summer will reap benefits that stay with you – even if it is just additional vitamin D. When I do this practice in summer, I often think of the term "Apollo-blessed" and it is hard not to think of the benevolence of a sun god when enjoying the real beauty of summer. If it is colder when you do this, pay attention to the cooling air in your lungs and on your skin. Sun on a cold winter's day is as welcome as it is in summer because it gives you hope even in the midst of the season's chill. Try to feel for where in your body you are holding tension and try to release that feeling whether by tensing and releasing or by gently stroking the area.

Another way to put yourself in tune with the season's effects on your body is to improve communication with your body. You can get clues from your dreams and from the world around you. Do you find yourself always running around in a maze, utterly terrified, in your dreams? Do you find that you often face travel problems when you undertake your daily commute? Perhaps, on a subconscious level, your body is trying to tell you that you've lost your way and need to slow down and re-think things? I am blessed with a splendid medical doctor who often says completely bizarre things that shock me into thinking outside the box. His most recent response to my Repetitive Strain Injury problems brought on by too much texting was "Why don't you stop texting then?" Good point.

The fact is your body wants to be healthy and wants you to enjoy great health. It has a vested interest in making you comfortable and happy. Most illnesses arise from your body misunderstanding what is good for you – or why you're doing what you're doing. If you cancel one holiday too many to get up to date with work, you find your body rebels and makes you ill so that you have an enforced break, which regrettably doesn't feel much like a holiday.

I am big on walking around barefoot, something which must drive my slipper-buying family members mad, as I will have perfectly good slippers to hand and still wander about unshod. I was told by a friend who even walks outside barefoot (see box) that we have reflexology points in our feet and they are stimulated by the different surfaces you get when you walk around without shoes on. There is also a great benefit to walking on the cool earth beneath your feet.

"Sun on a cold winter's day is as welcome as it is in summer because it gives you hope even in the midst of the season's chill."

RITUAL

Barefoot walking

This is a great ritual to do in your back garden, but if you don't have one or you prefer connecting to wilder nature, take yourself off to a forest or wood and really let nature into your life. Even a local park holds the same delights of feeling cool soil and soft grass under your feet. The cult movie *Pretty Woman* showed Richard Gere stepping away from his corporate office to go walking barefoot in the park. In doing so, he realised he wanted to build and save companies rather than break them up after hostile takeovers. You may well find that you come across a number of revelations about your life such as this when you are connected to the ground beneath your feet.

PREPARATION

You will need:
Just a little courage!

INTENTION

I walk the earth as nature intended and am healed and whole.

RITUAL STEPS

1 Remove your shoes and set them aside.
2 Take three deep cleansing breaths, in and out through your nose.
3 State your intention, either using the one given above or creating your own one, as long as it is positive and in the present tense.
4 Stand up and walk a short distance with intent, remembering to put your feet flat against the ground. Feel the earth beneath you. Are you comfortable with the textures you feel underfoot? If you're in a wooded area, are there twigs under your feet making things uncomfortable? Can you walk elsewhere that is more comfortable?
5 Let the scent of the grass or forest floor fill your lungs and pay attention to the thoughts that come up as you walk.
6 If you find that your mind has gone blank, enjoy that sensation of a quietened mind too.

JOURNAL REFLECTIONS

Reflect on how walking barefoot made you feel. Were you happy to do it or could you not wait to get your shoes back on? Did you think that others would be judging you? Did you judge yourself for doing it? Is being judged by others something you often worry about? If so, when in particular? Did you get any insight from the action of walking barefoot in public or indeed just in your garden? What images flashed into your mind?

RITUALISE IT

Do this ritual as often as you can. Obviously there are seasons in which it is easier, but I have even walked barefoot in winter (don't do this if you're frail or susceptible to colds). A regular reconnection to the earth is one of the best ways to feel grounded and calm.

DAILY BENEFIT

You will find as you progress in this ritual that you almost begin an open communication with the earth and get a sort of bio-feedback loop, in which your intuition opens up and tells you what you need to know at this time in your life. You will also become more sure-footed when you're back in shoes. This ritual gives you structure and a foundation that you can take with you into your everyday life.

MY BAREFOOTED FRIEND

I once walked to the local shops with a friend of mine who goes everywhere barefoot. The local teenagers had a grand old time calling him a "dirty hippie" and he had a brilliant time responding: 'At least I'm old enough to buy booze, saddos.' He literally had no shame or embarrassment in wearing no shoes. He would often get banned from supermarkets due to "health and safety", but it was all water off a duck's back. I once, on a whim, decided to go barefoot with him. I almost died of embarrassment, but then felt a surge of satisfaction when I got back indoors. I had conquered my fear of what other people think (at least a little). It can be useful to break with convention every once in a while, as long as no one gets hurt.

6

RITUALS TO LIVE BY

*"You have to know your triggers for stress and then
have rituals for combating them."*
Gabrielle Bernstein, life coach and author

I've drawn on the rituals from the earlier chapters to create powerful practices that form touchstones in your day, week, month, and year. The aim is for you to build up a number of comforting, calming rituals that support you whenever you need them. Sometimes you have daily tasks that can't be avoided and you can build up a sense of dread around doing them. Here we learn how to use the power of ritual to make these daily duties far more relaxing and enjoyable, turning them into a source of pleasure instead of stress. Remember: Your sense of sight can allow you to look upon things that instil a greater feeling of serenity. Your sense of sound can allow you to block out the noise and enjoy a transporting experience. Your sense of smell can align you to more calming times. Your sense of taste can give you pleasure and comfort you. Your sense of touch is soothing and immediate.

Daily Rituals

Each day is a gift but when it is pouring with rain and grumpy commuters are all you can see, it may be hard to remember that. Starting and ending your day with certain rituals will allow it to flow more naturally and keep you in a state of grace. At the end of the daily rituals, I have included suggestions for your journalling session – it is up to you whether you write your journal in the mornings or the evenings. Do what works best for you.

LETTING GO OF PERFECTION

The best thing that ever happened to improve my mental health was to accept that things would never be perfect. I came to this realisation the hard way. I strove for perfection in everything I did, from writing to cleaning, and often found myself in the pit of despair when I couldn't meet the high standards I'd set myself. I eventually came to realise that a beautifully made bed has to be slept in and remade the next day. You can't dust your home and preserve it in aspic so that no further dust is ever created. Everything is cyclical and ever-changing and the only way to be in the world is to learn to flow within it.

Whenever my OCD used to get too much, my therapist would ask me to return to the breath – to allow my looping thoughts to calm down by just paying attention to the in and out of my breath. I would still myself and close my eyes to stop visual stimuli careening me down the path of what needed doing. This also led me to use my senses more and more in my healing – I discovered that I could stop myself falling down the hole of stress and worry by tuning in to the anchoring quality of my senses.

RITUAL

Starting your day

Since you have to brush your teeth and wash your face in the morning anyway, why not make it into a ritual? My aunt has a religious practice in which she splashes water on her face and asks God to give her light to see clearly. You don't have to be religious to ask for things to go well in your day. When you voice your desire and your intent to have a good day, your subconscious listens and then conspires to make it so. It can be a purely secular act.

PREPARATION

You will need:
Bathroom toiletries

INTENTION

My day runs smoothly and gracefully.

RITUAL STEPS

1 Begin your day with three deep breaths in and out through the nose.
2 State the intention given above or devise your own, but keep it simple, positive, and present.
3 Say exactly what you're doing with each act of your morning ablutions so you know why you're doing it. For example, you could say, 'I am honouring my teeth and making them strong and healthy' as you begin brushing your teeth; 'I am giving myself the gift of clear sight' as you put in your contact lenses; 'I am keeping my skin clean and healthy' when you wash your face.

4 When you step into the shower, practise a bit of self-massage by allowing the water to fall for a while on your tight shoulders and groggy head.

5 Remember to lovingly moisturise your body after your shower, ensuring you have woken up early enough to really take your time over this step.

6 If you blow dry your hair, really enjoy the sensation of hot air on your skin.

7 Lay out the clothes you want to change into when you return from work in the evening.

8 Begin your day with gratitude for your unique circumstance and life, blessing all the people who are around you.

BENEFIT

This ritual adds a dimension of self-care into your morning routine. If you do it regularly, you will learn how beneficial it is to your well-being, and be less likely to sleep in and miss out any part of it.

RITUAL

Commuting well

Whether you're stuck in traffic or compressed into a train carriage, commuting can be the most stressful part the day. However, with a little careful planning it is possible to make this unpleasant task another wonderful part of your day, full of sensory pleasures.

PREPARATION

You will need:
Bag packed the night before
Clothes laid out the night before

INTENTION

I travel mindfully and reach my destination relaxed and calm.

RITUAL STEPS

1 Wake up early enough to leave the house on time. If possible, leave a bit earlier and avoid the commuter rush.
2 Take three deep cleansing breaths, in and out through your nose, as you leave your house. Begin with the intent of having a wonderfully relaxing commute in to work.
3 State your intention: either use the example given above or devise your own.
4 Be truly present in your commute. We try to make ourselves absent with music or books or newspapers, but you'd be surprised how much you notice if you keep your eyes and ears open. The universe often has some wonderful surprises in store such as a poster for a gig you really want to go to or a friend you haven't seen in years. Pay attention to colours around you and really notice details that you might miss normally. For example, do you know the name of the company that makes the panels for your train carriage? I do because I have seen the logo on the floor of the carriage panel. Your mind will begin to consider all the industry and effort that went into creating the system that you're currently using to get to work. Really marvel at the wonders around you and the blessings we enjoy each day of our lives.

BENEFIT

The commute becomes more of an opportunity to see your
world with fresh eyes, not something you dread, and you will
begin your day in a more positive frame of mind.

RITUAL

Lunchtime break

Make your lunch a real break. Step away from your place
of work and get out into the fresh air – yes, even in winter.
Really get to know the area you work in. If you are unlucky
enough to be based on an industrial estate in the middle of
nowhere, download some truly inspiring TV shows to watch
in your break, either comedies to cheer you up or dramas set
in stunning locations to take you out of your everyday world.
Try to connect with colleagues if you can. A shared lunch is
a point of connection that is great for both your physical and
mental health. Plus you might discover some amazing people
with lots to say for themselves.

PREPARATION

You will need:
Pre-packed lunch
Craft items
Book
Headphones and a mobile phone/tablet

INTENTION

I nourish myself with delicious food, enjoy a proper break, and make good use of my time.

RITUAL STEPS

1 Even at work, remember to take your three deep cleansing breaths. This will remind your brain that you are now entering ritual mode and must be more mindful and relaxed.

2 State your intention either out loud or in your mind, if that feels more comfortable for you.

3 Eat your lunch mindfully (see page 105). Step away from your desk and sit somewhere comfortable to enjoy every mouthful properly. Really taste your food and appreciate each ingredient in your meal.

4 Take your full hour – don't rush back to your desk. It will all be there for you whenever you get back. Take in some crafts to do if you're good with your hands or read a book (nothing work-related!) or watch a half-hour comedy on your phone. If you are watching something, make that only once or twice a week to avoid overdoing your screen time.

5 Try to incorporate a walk into your lunch hour. It is best to do this after you've eaten so you can digest your food while taking a gentle stroll.

6 Keep your senses alive to all that is happening around you and stay inquisitive to attract happy surprises to you.

BENEFIT

A proper lunch break is important for your digestion and stepping away from your desk is a really vital part of staying on top form when you are at work. When you take the time to eat mindfully, you chew your food better and enjoy it more. Fresh air at lunchtime will avoid the afternoon slump and you'll find your mood improves with the exercise a brisk walk gives you.

RITUAL

Easy evening

Setting up clear boundaries between your public and private life is what a good evening ritual is all about. You are getting rid of the stresses of the day and entering the calm haven that is your home. If that doesn't sound familiar, try doing this ritual for a while and see if you can start to get that feeling.

PREPARATION

You will need:
Loungewear laid out
Bath oil

INTENTION
I am relaxed and happy in my home.

RITUAL STEPS

1 Change your clothes as soon as you step through the door. Pick the most comfortable loungewear possible – a kaftan or yoga pants and a T-shirt, or be nude if that's your thing (though if you have kids, they might well send you their therapist's bill later in life). The point is that you are crossing the boundary from public working you to private domestic you. You are in your home and it is your haven.

2 Once you have changed, do three chores, no more. These can be anything at all and some suggestions are running a machine, making dinner, dealing with the mail, spending 15 minutes picking things up and putting them where they

belong, dusting, cleaning the toilet or loading/unloading the dishwasher. It doesn't matter what you do, just do no more than three. It is so that you don't have a huge backlog of chores when you should be enjoying your weekend.

3 Run yourself a hot bath and put in some really fragrant bath oil.

4 Lying in the bath, take three deep cleansing breaths in and out through the nose. Allow the water to ease away your aches and pains. Think about all that went well with your day and how you can replicate the experience the next day. Don't dwell on what didn't go right.

5 When you emerge, apply some moisturising cream to your body with care and then change back into your loungewear.

6 Eat your dinner mindfully with your family (see pages 107–108). Avoid drinking alcohol during the week if you can as it is dehydrating and will make you feel groggy the next day. It is also a depressive so if you're already feeling tired and grumpy from your working day, it will exacerbate those feelings.

7 After dinner, prepare your lunch for the next day and iron/lay out your clothes for the next day too.

8 Keep to a set time for bed and turn the lights down and start preparing for it about half an hour before you're actually in your bed. Try to avoid gadgets and TV in that time as well. This allows your body to know that sleep is coming and to start feeling a bit more tired.

9 While you may want to veg in front of your TV (and that is no bad thing), try every once in a while to do something different such as a yoga session at home (use videos if you don't know what to do) or a meditation – try to involve your family so that you all have something in common, but don't worry if they're not as enthusiastic.

BENEFIT

We all have things we have to do to make our days run smoother – chores and errands and other not-very-fun things. However, if you can get into the habit of having an evening ritual that nurtures you alongside all the dull stuff you have to do, you will find that your days and nights run far more smoothly. Above all, you will feel in control of your day and that is the first step towards feeling calmer.

JOURNAL REFLECTIONS

1 It can help to write out a routine for your morning and evening, until you memorise it completely. It helps to see in writing what you need to do and the process of getting it out of your head and onto paper is very calming.

2 Write down five interesting things you saw on your commute to work. It could be beautiful buildings or well-dressed people. It might be a poster for a film you want to see or an exhibition that is coming to town. Write down the details here and try to plan it in to visit either the building (if it is open to the public) or the film or exhibition. Such happy insights will make your commute an endless source of pleasure instead of something to endure.

3 Write down a series of things you can achieve or enjoy in half an hour. It could be a mini-yoga session or learning to crochet. Once you have your list, pick one or two things from it each week to make your daily lunch breaks more interesting.

Weekly Rituals

My mother-in-law grew up in the 1950s when there were specific days for doing certain chores. She told me that all the ladies would be out cleaning their windows on a Wednesday morning, the gardening was done on a particular day and, of course, there was "bin day". The rhythm of life was in those shared weekly tasks done together. It was a social cohesion that seems very alien to our modern eyes. We like individuality and we do things when we want to do them – or never, which is also fine. However, if you do enjoy the certainty of ritual then a weekly one is often more achievable than a daily one. Incidentally, don't beat yourself up if you *don't* manage to do something. We are born to enjoy our lives and do what makes us happy, not follow rules and regulations and make rods for our backs, so if a ritual is feeling like a chore and a pressure, then make adjustments.

RITUAL

Weekly rhythm

From the working week to our weekend rest, we have a lot to pack in to those seven days. From housework to social commitments and miscellaneous errands, each week can go by in a blur if we don't take time to set a rhythm and stick to it. The weekend is a relatively new invention, having been introduced at the Ford automobile company in 1926. Other car manufacturers were forced to follow suit to avoid losing workers to Ford. This concept then made it across the Atlantic to Britain, where traditionally most people might have only had an afternoon off a week. Our luxurious two-day break never seems long enough, but it must have seemed to last forever when it was first introduced to people used to working long hours with little time off. To say nothing of the evenings we get during the week to ourselves. In fact, we do have plenty of time to get everything done – we just don't establish the rhythm we need to make it all run smoothly.

PREPARATION

You will need:
Family planner calendar

INTENTION
I enjoy the rhythm of my week and use it to make me feel happy and relaxed.

RITUAL STEPS
1 Set a rhythm for your week. Establish some markers, such as how many days in the week you're willing to socialise and whether there are any non-negotiable family or religious commitments that need to go on your weekly calendar. Mark them all in so you begin to get an overview of your week and how much time you have left for everything else.

2 If you are in a couple, don't forget to add in a "date night" to connect with your romantic partner and spend some quality time together. This may not be weekly; it could be that you can only afford childminding once a fortnight or every three weeks. Either way, mark it into the family planner calendar and make sure you do it.

3 If either of you or your children have plans or classes, mark them off on the calendar too and put it up where everyone can access it. As soon as you agree to go somewhere or do something, enter it into that planner so everyone knows where they're at with commitments. If a month starts looking

too busy, turn things down as you must build in adequate rest time.

4   Mark in mooching time. Mooch is a verb that comes from the old French word *muchier*, to skulk. It means wandering around aimlessly or loitering. It basically means you don't have any firm plans of what to do and so you do whatever you want, when the mood takes you. I usually keep two mooching evenings a week and a four-hour window at the weekend too. My plants are often involved in my mooching as I'll pick off dead leaves or feed some of them or re-pot some of them (see page 120).

5   Remember those three daily chores we had in the daily section (pages 144–146)? Your mooching time is also a good time to do other chores in a leisurely way. I don't mean full-on spring cleaning, but this is the time to ensure you have clean clothes for the coming week and that you are happy with the state of your bathroom. Your sense of smell will thank you if you can bathe in a serene spa-like haven over the coming week.

6   Once a week, schedule in a family meal to connect with your loved ones. Prepare the food mindfully as an expression of your love for them and get the little ones to help too so they can build skills as well as give you some much-needed help. Make these meals leisurely affairs so that you gain a real sense of connection.

BENEFITS

Each of these touchstones in a week nourishes your soul in some way. Whether it is connection with family or good food or just ambling around, you should build in such activities into the rhythm of your week in order to truly enjoy your leisure time and stay refreshed and calm at work.

RITUAL

Restorative rest

I view this as the most important ritual of the week. You should make time for a proper rest, whether that's napping post-lunch in front of the TV on a Sunday or having a wee lie-down in the middle of the day on Saturday. I am not keen on napping so my rest is having a couple of hours to myself enjoying a cup of tea and a good book. If I can get someone else to keep me supplied with those teas, so I don't have to get up from my perch, all the better. It is a good way to round off the weekend and get rid of Sunday night blues.

PREPARATION

You will need:
Blanket
A place where you won't be disturbed

INTENTION
I heal myself with rest and the gift of time.

RITUAL STEPS
1 Ask your family not to disturb you for an hour or so. If you have a room you can go to that is quiet and away from noise, such as a back bedroom, take yourself off to it.
2 Wrap yourself in the blanket.
3 Take three deep cleansing breaths in and out through your nose.
4 State your intention, either the one above or another that feels more geared to your aims specifically.

5   Lie or sit comfortably with your feet either stretched out in
    front of you or flat on the floor if you are sitting.
6   Take your attention to your body and do a scan of anywhere
    that feels tight or achy.
7   Stretch that part of your body if you can.
8   Close your eyes and keep gently breathing in and out
    through your nose.
9   Feel your body relaxing bit by bit. Snuggle down into
    the blanket if it feels more comfortable as your body
    temperature will drop when you are relaxing like this.
10 If you fall asleep, make it a power nap of half an hour or so.
    Any longer and you may feel groggy and interrupt your
    sleep pattern for later that night.
11 Once you're done with your ritual of rest, make a soothing
    drink and some noise with your family.

BENEFIT

Intentional rest gets rid of the one thing that is the enemy
of true calm – guilt! We often feel as though we should be
doing something when we're just resting. It feels lazy and
unproductive to just sit there. If you ritualise the act of
resting, it becomes a sort of "doing" and you give yourself
permission to take yourself off for a considered rather than
slapdash rest. Over time, as your guilt gets increasingly under
control, you will find you don't need to go to a special place
to enjoy rest and will be able to do it more and more.

JOURNAL REFLECTIONS

Write down three priorities for your week. Are you keen
on having a cleaner house? Want to spend more time with
your siblings? Want to do more fun stuff with your partner
or kids? Select three goals that match your priorities and put

them into your weekly schedule. If spending time doing fun stuff with the kids is your priority, maybe mark in that you'll take them swimming or to a zip line at the weekend. If you want a cleaner house, schedule in a cleaning blitz of a whole day at the weekend or book a cleaner if it is unfeasible that you'll get the time to do it. If you want to spend time with your siblings, get in touch and make it happen.

Monthly Rituals

Monthly rituals can sound daunting because of the enormity of the task, such as balancing our books or cleaning the oven. However, the more you stick to a monthly ritual with such things, the more it will become second nature and no longer a source of stress. If you know exactly what is coming up in a given month, you can react to it without panic or discomfort.

RITUAL

Window cleaning

Dirty windows are a great metaphor for not being able to see your way clearly. Oddly enough, if you clean just this aspect of your home's structure, you often find that you gain clarity in any aspect of life that has been eluding you. Because I have a tiny home, I do this once a month for all my windows, but if you have a larger home, only do it for one of the rooms in your property per month, going around each one until you have done them all. If you have mobility issues, pay someone to come and do the window cleaning but do get it done.

PREPARATION

You will need:
Bucket of hot soapy water
Couple of drops of essential oil
Sponge
Squeegee or newspaper

INTENTION
The windows of my home are as clean and sparkling as my path ahead.

RITUAL STEPS
1   Take three deep cleansing breaths in and out through your nose and then state your intention, either as above or your own.
2   Choose to clean the windows in one room, inside and out.
3   Metaphorically the windows are the eyes of your home and they are where you get light and air. It makes sense to keep this part of your home clean and clear so that you can symbolically and actually look out and see what's what.
4   You can engage your sense of smell by using essential oils in your cleaning water so that when the sun hits your windows, you get a delicate hint of aroma from the oils you used. Select the oils that you like best and add to a bucket of warm, soapy water.
5   Inhale deeply the scented water as you clean the windows. Imagine that as you are cleansing the dirt, you are also ridding yourself of any situation that no longer serves you.

Tip: If you really want a smear-free finish, use old newspaper to buff the wet windows and really get a sparkle going.

JOURNAL REFLECTIONS

Make a note of where in your life you begin to see a shift as soon as your windows are clean. You may find that cleaning your bedroom windows gives you greater clarity in your relationships and that cleaning kitchen windows reveals specific dietary needs that you didn't know you had. This isn't as spooky as it sounds – it is simply your subconscious looking out for metaphors in your life and manifesting answers according to the cleaning of the relevant spaces.

BENEFIT

Apart from benefiting from more light and less dust, clean windows enable you to move forward in life as your path becomes clearer and you can see what your next move should be. The aroma you get from your clean windows will also relax you and make you feel more cosseted at home.

RITUAL

Monthly meet-up

Schedule in a monthly meet-up with friends who really uplift and support you. We are often so busy in our daily lives that friendships can fall to the wayside, but having a monthly date in the diary when you have told all the pals you like where you will be ensures that you get to see them far more regularly. You will find that more and more of your friends will try to make a regular monthly meet-up than they would if you play diary ping-pong with them all once a month.

PREPARATION

You will need:
Possibly a Whatsapp group or Facebook private event
Convenient venue
Calendar

INTENTION
I make time to see the friends who uplift and support me.

RITUAL STEPS
1 Using the technology that your friends are most used to, set up a regular group meeting on the day that is most convenient for most of you. It could be the first Saturday of the month or the last Friday. Just keep it consistent so everyone knows when it is each month.
2 State your intention as you set up the group so you know clearly why you're doing it. You could even add the intention to the group chat info, if you think it appropriate and as long as no one feels it is a passive-aggressive statement on anyone who doesn't make the time!
3 Pick a venue that is handy for most of your friends.
4 Set a time and make sure you're there for the first one.
5 Establish the rule that no one gets berated for not making it in any given month – it is a standing arrangement that you all do your best to attend, but if you can't make it then so be it. When the pressure of a regular meet-up is taken away like that, you often find that people will make more of an effort.
6 If you find one month that only you turn up for a meeting, don't sweat it, have a drink and then head on home. There are bound to be several who turn up the following month.

7   Keep things light and cheery and aim to walk away from
    the night feeling happy and relaxed. If that happens enough
    times, you'll all look forward to it as a monthly ritual of
    renewal.

JOURNAL REFLECTIONS

Make a list of the friends who always make you feel
great about yourself. The ones who are funny or kind or
generous and big-hearted. These are the folks you want in
your monthly meet-up group. If you know someone who
always complains and is often on a bit of a downer, invite
them as well, but let the group carry him or her up rather than
be dragged downwards with negativity. The group dynamic
can be a force for good if enough of you are on the right page.

BENEFIT

Friendships are essential to good mental health and you
will naturally feel calmer and more relaxed when you have
good, deep connections. Build this with the people you love
through regular sessions of chat and laughter and you will
always have a support network to call upon when things get
a bit rough. After all, if you're all there for each other in the
good times, you know you'll also be able to cheer each other
up in the bad times.

Seasonal Rituals

Every season has its rituals, depending on where you live,
the family you have, the religion you follow. Seasonal rituals
help us connect as a community of friends and family.

We all know that one friend who throws the best BBQ of the summer season. Perhaps you all get together to watch a sports event at a big party each year or your house is the best haunted one on Halloween. A lot of these holidays and rites of passage are not just marketing opportunities – they mean something to the people who enjoy them. They are an opportunity to feel connected and loved. If you have nothing that gives you that feeling, create it yourself and begin new seasonal traditions.

RITUAL

Spring clean

Now don't groan and ask what this has to do with creating calm and connecting with people. I defy you to relax in a dirty and disorganised home. Even if you feel quite comfortable in a messy home, every once in a while it is good to shake up the energy and get it flowing again. Historically, people used to spring clean to stay healthy. The dust and germs that had to be trapped indoors over the cold winter, when windows were shut to keep the heat in, had to be cleared from the house. Windows and doors were thrown open, rugs were taken out and beaten on lines, floors were swept and light fixtures dusted. Having a similar ritual of shaking out the energy of your home once a year is a great way to combat stress and also to feel like you're doing something. Sometimes we can feel stuck in a job or a relationship that isn't going anywhere and a good clear-out gives us the mental space to think about what we really want.

Plus it is a great way to prepare for the smudging ritual in Chapter 3 (see pages 73–75).

PREPARATION

You will need:
Cleaning supplies
Elbow grease

INTENTION

My home is my haven of calm and rest.

RITUAL STEPS

1   Book yourself a good two to three days for your spring clean. It is an annual deep-clean event and so will take longer than your usual weekend blitz. Mark it out on the calendar and get your family on board to help.

2   State your intention when you begin, before you've done anything else. If you would rather have a different intention than the one above, that's fine, but make it positive and present.

3   Go from room to room in your house and make a list of all the chores that need doing. This might range from decluttering a particular drawer to fixing a wardrobe door or steam-cleaning a carpet. Gather all the jobs, big and small, onto one master list.

4   Divide that master list into room lists and hand over a room each to the appropriate family member. Don't try to do it all yourself – that way stress lies!

5   Clear your clutter – especially before big events such as house moves or weddings. Make three piles: things to keep

and organise; things to give away or throw; things to sell. Then put the charity things in your car boot immediately and list the things to sell immediately. If you leave it till later, you might not get to it.

6 Use your thoughts to help you. Is there something that has always caused you to think, 'I must do something about that'? Personally, I feel this way every time I look at my oven as it is used daily but hardly ever thoroughly cleaned. As part of my spring cleaning, I always put money aside for a professional valet of my oven. Since it is a high-use item, I feel that it is worth it. For weeks afterwards, I feel a sense of calm when I look at the oven as I know I have dealt with that irritant. It may be a pile of newspapers for you. Or a broken drawer. Take this opportunity to remove the annoyance from your life.

7 Set about cleaning what is left in a complete, methodical way. You will find that you quickly get into a rhythm. Take regular breaks and ensure that you take your three cleansing breaths regularly as you go through each task.

JOURNAL REFLECTIONS

Reflect on how it felt to spring clean. When you have finished and are sitting looking at your beautiful space, write down a set of goals for your year ahead. How will you keep things calm and ordered in your life? Will you hire a cleaner to come weekly or will you start a chart of chores with stickers for your kids so that you get more consistent help? Think about what will make you feel calmer and in control over the coming year and write it down. You may need to get agreement from others in your family to implement all your changes but make a start by at least evaluating what needs to happen to keep you in this happy place.

BENEFITS

From cobwebs to unused items, many things accumulate in our space without us being aware of them. A proper spring clean helps you get back control from the encroaching clutter and mayhem. You start the wheel of the year feeling calm and serene.

RITUAL

Summer solstice

Each year I used to go to Pendle Hill in the UK for a festival that would celebrate the longest day of the year – the summer solstice. The weather – being Lancashire in the north of England – was not always as warm as it could be, but the atmosphere was always incredibly welcoming. You too can enjoy a ritual at the height of summer by celebrating the light that is at its zenith before it begins its ebb away again towards winter. You can commit to the fires of summer anything that is not for your highest good.

PREPARATION

You will need:
Slips of paper
Fire pit or fireproof dish
Jug of water

INTENTION

I release all that no longer serves me.

RITUAL STEPS

1 Take three breaths in and out through your nose.

2 Light the fire. If you have an outdoor firepit, all the better. Light it at midday when the sun is high in the sky. If you don't have a firepit, put a fireproof bowl on a fireproof surface.

3 State your intention, either the one above or one that feels more appropriate to you.

4 Take the slips of paper you have put aside and write on each something that you no longer want in your life. For example, you could write "debt" or "noisy neighbours".

5 Then take the slip of paper and either burn it in your firepit, imagining the problem leaving your life in a perfect way, or carefully burn the paper and drop it into the fireproof bowl. Have your jug of water on standby in case of any accidents.

6 Enjoy the smell of the fire and the sensation of heat coming off it and the mid day sun.

7 When you have burned up all your troubles, sit or stand still for a while in front of the fire, appreciating all the warmth and nurturing it gives us in life.

JOURNAL REFLECTIONS

Imagine that a genie had given you three wishes. Write out what those three wishes would be. Then, imagine that you had to work for those three wishes. Break down what you would need to do over the course of a year, a month, a week, *today* to make that wish come true. Take one tiny step towards realising these miraculous dreams.

BENEFIT

It is useful to know what it is you don't want as much as what it is that you do want. By first burning the things you want to remove and then writing out the things you want to attract, you will find that you begin to clarify in your own mind where you want things to go in your near future. Your mind will then begin to make plans to have those things come to pass. It can feel magical, but it is very natural.

RITUAL

Autumn spice

The best thing about the end of summer is the scent of spices that fills kitchens and restaurants. From October's pumpkin spice lattes to hearty stews throughout autumn, the aromatics of this season are a heavenly treat. You can learn to enliven your taste buds with spicy treats at home and add some pizzazz to your morning mug with a spicy chai instead of coffee. You can also introduce some calming spices such as nutmeg and cardamom.

PREPARATION

You will need:
Cardamom pods
Cinnamon stick
Loose tea leaves
Full-fat milk
Sugar to taste
Fresh nutmeg

INTENTION
I nourish my body with the spices that warm it in the chill of autumn.

RITUAL STEPS

1 Much like in the tea ritual on pages 96–99, prepare to make a special, nourishing cup of tea. Take your three cleansing breaths in and out through the nose.

2 State your intention, either the one above or another that is positive and present.

3 Then put some milk in a pan – measure it out in mugs according to how many people you are making it for.

4 Drop a cinnamon stick and three or four cardamom pods into the milk.

5 Add a heaped tablespoon of loose tea per person.

6 Leave the tea to brew up under a medium heat on the stove.

7 Strain into mugs once the colour has changed to that of a pleasantly strong tea.

8 Add sugar as required and grate a little nutmeg over the top.

JOURNAL REFLECTIONS

Reflect on how this ritual felt for you. What feelings did it bring up and why? Which spices remind you of your childhood? What recipes were they in? Do you have any particular memories around cooler weather and spicy foods and drinks? Write down what you remember and see if you can recreate them this autumn.

BENEFIT

Cardamom is great for the digestion and cinnamon has been used in treating bronchitis. Nutmeg helps with rheumatism. All these spices may be wonderful for your health, but, more importantly, they appeal to your senses and the smell can calm you down and make you feel relaxed. When the rain of autumn has begun, turning to spices can stop you feeling miserable and defeated by the weather.

RITUAL

Winter warmth

Winter is a magical pause in the year. It also contains
the biggest holiday of the year in the Western world –
Christmas. Its preceding celebration was the Roman
festival of feasting in December called Saturnalia. It
is a time of fairy lights, the sound of jingling bells, the
scent of pine and cinnamon, the taste of mulled wine,
and the feel of soft woollen socks. It is an occasion
for comfort and calm at home and, yet, we often run
ourselves ragged at this time of year. We feel the need to
do endless shopping, to engage in overconsumption, to
lay our expectations on others and on ourselves, and to
weep if it isn't like in the movies. This year, let go of your
expectations regarding the holidays and promise yourself
a stress-free winter cuddling up at home with fewer
commitments and fewer dramas. You can still connect with
your loved ones through the wonderful tradition of card-
sending. You may find the idea of writing lots of cards
exhausting and stressful, but it can actually be a great
way to express your love and appreciation for your family
and friends, especially if you make it a delightful annual
ritual.

PREPARATION

Set aside a number of nights in the lead up to Christmas in
order to write out your cards. Look forward to it as a comfy
night in with some treats and a chance to chat – albeit in
written form – to your nearest and dearest.

You will need:

Bottle of mulled wine (optional)

Mince pies (optional)

Christmas/Winter's Greeting cards

Stamps

Soft woolly socks

INTENTION

I embrace all the sensual delights of Saturnalia and send messages of hope and love through my greetings cards.

RITUAL STEPS

1 Pop on your woolly socks and warm up your mulled wine or have a hot chocolate with nutmeg. The mince pie is also optional but I highly recommend it.

2 Lay out your cards and get your address book out.

3 State your intention or one that is closer to what you want to achieve with this ritual.

4 Put on some music – I love Billie Holliday as hearing her voice just makes me think of wintertime.

5 Begin your evening's work with three deep cleansing breaths in and out through the nose. You can start this process in November if you're super-organised and just send all your cards out on the 1st of December. If not, don't worry, any time in winter is great – even belated ones in January.

6 Write out a couple of cards a night, taking care to really think about the people you are sending them to – don't do any card out of obligation, but because you really miss the connection with that person. Make each card personal and give a bit of your news. Your cards shouldn't be hurried,

dutiful affairs but actually talk about what has happened in the previous year.

7 As you seal each envelope, say a blessing for the person over it. This seals your ritual, but it also puts out into the universe that you are thinking good thoughts for that person.

JOURNAL REFLECTIONS

Make a note of things you wrote about the most when writing to your friends. What has really impacted you this year? Was it more funny things or was there some sadness there? What would you like to be able to write about in next year's cards? Writing out your hopes and wishes will make them more real for you and you can check back in a year's time to see if you managed to achieve all that you had hoped for.

BENEFIT

With all the hoo-ha surrounding the behemoth celebration that is Christmas, it is good to concentrate on just one tradition and do it well. All the winter celebrations are about connection with family and friends and nothing says that you miss someone more than a handwritten note that is more than just a basic greeting. As to all the other trimmings and demands of the winter season, get your family on board to help and remember to keep perspective. It is meant to be fun, not perfect.

FINAL REFLECTIONS

Instead of New Year resolutions, write down old year learnings. What have you discovered about yourself over the course of doing the rituals in this book? What are your stress triggers? What immediately makes you feel calmer. If you can, try to isolate one ritual for each sense so that you have something to hand at all times. As an example, mine are:

Sight – I have beach screensavers on my work computer, home computer, and mobile screen. That way if I need to see a calming scene, I have only to turn to the screen nearest to me at that time.

Sound – I take wireless headphones with me whenever I am away from home so that if I begin to hear very discordant sounds, I can pop them on and listen to something more soothing.

Smell – I use a coconut-based lotion and normally only need to put my nose down to my arm to be comforted by the smell. However, I also have a scented lip balm and an aromatherapy stick in my drawer at work.

Taste – I know both the smell and the taste of Earl Grey tea makes me feel secure and protected so I keep a box of it on my desk and another at home.

Touch – I massage my upper shoulders whenever I begin to feel stressed and that immediately makes me feel better.

CONCLUSION

*"A ritual is the enactment of a myth. And, by
participating in the ritual, you are participating
in the myth. And since myth is a projection of the
depth wisdom of the psyche, by participating in a
ritual, participating in the myth, you are being, as it
were, put in accord with that wisdom, which is the
wisdom that is inherent within you anyhow. Your
consciousness is being re-minded of the wisdom of
your own life. I think ritual is terribly important."*
Joseph Campbell, author of *The Hero With A Thousand Faces*

The most amazing part of writing this book has been the research into the senses, which has alerted me to how far they are blended. Taste is as important as texture when deciding if we like eating something. Smell and taste merge to give a more complete picture as do hearing and touch. The mammoth amount of information given to us by our sight then informs all the other senses about what to expect.

When I was a food and drink editor, I remember the birth of molecular gastronomy, along with chefs who would playfully subvert our ideas of what to expect when we popped what looked like a sweet fruit into our mouths only to find it was a savoury delight, like a chicken parfait. I won't lie: I hated it. While the food may have been delicious and the skill and techniques impressive, I like my senses working as they should. I don't want to trick them. I remember as a child despising beetroot for no other reason than the very deceit of it – it looked a bright colour and stained my fingers a pleasing pink so why didn't it taste of strawberries or blancmange? Its vegetal taste was a betrayal in my eyes.

Our senses are there as allies and not tricksters. We can rely on them to tell us if we like or dislike something, if we feel good or bad, even if we are on the edge of a breakdown. Five years ago, my husband suffered a nervous breakdown. Stress and unhappiness at work combined with residual depression over a series of family deaths caused his body to shut down. He told me that he first realised things were very, very wrong when he couldn't taste things properly and he had to keep moistening his lips because his mouth was always dry. He found he could have intense conversations, but was not making eye contact with the person he was talking to because some deeper part of him had checked out. We ask people to look at us when we want their attention because we know that this is a sign that they are truly present.

Thankfully he has now largely recovered, mostly through quitting his high-stress job and using herbal medicines. The first thing that made him realise he'd turned a corner was tasting his food again. Now dinner is a ritual, a real pleasure with a set table and a pause in the day. We make eye contact and there are no screens at the table (unless *The Great British Bake Off* is on, of course, in which case the ritual moves to the sofa and the plates to our laps).

Coming so close to knowing how bad things can get when you're not able to tap into a sense of calm within you has made me extra-cautious about not overdoing it and learning to relax. My sister still says she doesn't know why I feel the need to be like a jack-in-the-box, leaping up to do things when I could be slouching on the couch. Thankfully I've learnt to know my limits and no longer push past them. I only leap up to do something if I feel like doing it, not because of a nagging voice in my head or an unhappy pressure to do so.

My senses have helped me in that endeavour and it has resulted in this book. I am an unashamed sensualist and take my pleasure in many things that I experience daily through my senses. I hope, as you have worked through the rituals, that you have begun to feel more connected with your own five senses. The whole point of ritual is to make you feel better and more connected, which is why I encourage you to make up your own instead of just relying on the ones you can find here. Now that you know the principles of how rituals appeal to all our senses, I hope you can create ones that are very personal to you. I wish you well on that journey to a calmer, happier you.

ACKNOWLEDGEMENTS

Thank you to Jo Lal, Rachel Gregory, Bethony James and the team at Tigger Publishing for making this book happen and to Dawn Bates for her excellent editing skills. Thanks also to Poorna Bell for reading the first draft and saying such lovely things about my writing. I'm also grateful to my teachers over the years, especially the late Ross Heaven who taught me so much about the art of ritual and friendship. Finally, thanks to my family and friends for their love and support – in particular to my husband Gary who has provided lots of snacks, drinks, foot massages and encouragement in the course of me writing this book.

CONNECT WITH THE AUTHOR

Website: taniaahsan.co.uk
Instagram: @everydaycalmingrituals
Twitter: @calmingrituals

TriggerHub.org is one of the most elite and scientifically proven forms of mental health intervention

Trigger Publishing is the leading independent mental health and wellbeing publisher in the UK and US. Clinical and scientific research conducted by assistant professor Dr Kristin Kosyluk and her highly acclaimed team in the Department of Mental Health Law & Policy at the University of South Florida (USF), as well as complementary research by her peers across the US, has independently verified the power of lived experience as a core component in achieving mental health prosperity. Specifically, the lived experiences contained within our bibliotherapeutic books are intrinsic elements in reducing stigma, making those with poor mental health feel less alone, providing the privacy they need to heal, ensuring they know the essential steps to kick-start their own journeys to recovery, and providing hope and inspiration when they need it most.

Delivered through TriggerHub, our unique online portal and accompanying smartphone app, we make our library of bibliotherapeutic titles and other vital resources accessible to individuals and organizations anywhere, at any time and with complete privacy, a crucial element of recovery. As such, TriggerHub is the primary recommendation across the UK and US for the delivery of lived experiences.

At Trigger Publishing and TriggerHub, we proudly lead the way in making the unseen become seen. We are dedicated to humanizing mental health, breaking stigma and challenging outdated societal values to create real action and impact. Find out more about our world-leading work with lived experience and bibliotherapy via triggerhub. org, or by joining us on:

🐦 @triggerhub_

🅕 @triggerhub.org

🅾 @triggerhub_

Printed in the USA
CPSIA information can be obtained
at www.ICGtesting.com
JSHW031714140824
68134JS00038B/3678